THE
FASHION ORACLE

*This book is dedicated to those
who choose to master their magic.*

THE
FASHION ORACLE

AN OCCULT GUIDE TO WHAT
TO WEAR INSPIRED BY CHANEL

NIEVE TIERNEY

WELBECK

CONTENTS

OPENING REFLECTIONS

A MESSAGE FROM NIEVE

Hello my loves,

The art of dressing is a layered experience – something Coco Chanel understood innately and instinctively mastered, shaped by her experiences in both fashion and life from her earliest days. The first consideration may be a practical one – choosing clothes that protect you from the elements and are appropriately chosen for the environment they will be seen in. Then, there is the more delicate decision of what identity we choose to step into and the personal narrative we wish to tell the world around us through our attire.

There is power in tapping into your vibration through the clothes you choose and clearly signalling an energy via your fashion choices.

For the fashion enthusiasts among us, our clothes go beyond practical utility. We recognize that our outfit choices define a visual identity and act as a code for the tribe to which we subscribe. But, are you aware there is an activation of energy in our sartorial choices? Did you know that colours carry frequency codes, and materials trigger an energy response when they touch your skin?

Coco Chanel understood that fashion transcends mere aesthetics. She wove in elements of numerology and astrology into her designs, infusing each creation with cosmic and personal significance – transforming her clothing into a true extension of her spirit.

As you connect with the archetypes within these pages, you will awaken their energy within you, embodying their guidance through the garments they recommend. These archetypes – inspired by the House of Chanel – draw from the brand's timeless wisdom and inspiration, for they embody the brand's legacy of strength, elegance and innovation.

When I speak about femininity and the impact Coco Chanel had on women's wardrobes, I'm referencing the broader context of her defiance against the rigid social structures of her era. Coco's journey was one of breaking down these barriers. As you work with the archetypes of this book I encourage you to honour the feminine aspects within yourself, regardless of how you identify – whether male, female or non-binary.

My wish and my prayer is that this book will empower you to connect with universal energy, as you are guided by the spirit and wisdom of Coco Chanel, Karl Lagerfeld and their successors – including Virginie Viard – in your fashion decisions. May it help you actualize the perfect energy solution and support you through the power of dressing.

With love,

COCO CHANEL

FASHION DISRUPTER, DESIGNER AND THE SECRET LANGUAGE OF HER ESOTERIC CODES.

The legendary Gabrielle "Coco" Chanel, an iconic disruptor of twentieth-century fashion, didn't just design clothes – she brought to life a revolutionary fashion vision that advanced the changing roles of women in society. Famous for her impeccable precision and exquisite craftsmanship, Coco forever altered the course of women's fashion by setting a new standard of modernity and luxury. Her designs were not only utterly chic but also empowering – a Chanel wardrobe acted as an equalizer, aligning with women's evolving aspirations to stand as equals to men.

This book explores Coco's well-documented interest in tarot and spiritual symbolism. She held a strong fascination with mystical and esoteric practices, including divination, astrology and numerology, which were deeply woven into the brand. Coco was known to use the Lenormand tarot deck for guidance in both her business decisions and personal matters. After her death these tarot cards were found at 31 rue Cambon – the heart of her fashion empire – frozen in time, symbolizing their importance in her life.

Once you walk up the spiralled mirrored staircase at 31 rue Cambon and enter Mademoiselle's Salon, you will find yourself surrounded by esoteric objects and spiritual symbols that Coco believed brought her protection and inspiration – her *objets* each telling a story. Lions (the emblems of her astrological rising star sign in Leo) command the room, from subtle motifs on furniture to

golden statues to a framed painting – all embodying their symbolism of strength, courage and royalty. Wheat (a symbol of abundance and prosperity in tarot) appears dried and artfully arranged on her mantelpiece, while a single stalk of wheat is immortalized in a painting by her dear friend Salvador Dalí. Each element speaks of Coco's deep connection to the mystical forces that shaped her life and legacy. As your eyes wander across the room, you'll see religious crosses, a bust of the goddess Aphrodite, Egyptian sphinxes, a Buddha, crystal balls, and a chandelier (designed by Coco herself) adorned with various crystals, orbs, stars, camellia flowers and clusters of grapes – each element a reflection of her spiritual interests.

It is believed that her interest in spiritual themes was sparked by Captain Arthur "Boy" Capel, her great love, who introduced her to literature and theosophy (a mystical philosophy that seeks knowledge of life's mysteries and the purpose of the universe). Moreover, Coco's openness to mystical guidance led her to consult with astrologers and clairvoyants throughout her life. She was said to have made decisions based on their advice, particularly when it came to business matters. These spiritual insights were also said to be part of her creative process, helping her to align her designs with the energies she believed were at play.

Coco's interest in the mystical world found its way into her collections in often subtle yet profound ways. Recurring motifs of lions, wheat, numerical symbols, and the camellia flower (representing purity and longevity) along with cosmic five-pointed stars, can be found repeatedly. Each, in turn, echoed her belief in the power of esoteric imagery. These elements contributed to the mystique and allure of the brand, infusing her designs with a deeper, almost magical quality. So, too, her consistent use of black and white – colours often associated with the duality of life and death, light and shadow – also reflects her understanding of the balance between opposites, another key theme in tarot. These symbols helped shape a brand that transcends fashion, touching on the spiritual and resonating with those who seek meaning beyond the material.

Coco's passion for tarot, numerology and esoteric themes was not just a personal interest – it was a fundamental part of her creative process and became part of the style lexicon at Chanel.

Karl Lagerfeld, the visionary successor to Coco, often drew on these mystical themes in his own designs. He was fascinated by ancient Egypt and drew inspiration from deities incorporating their symbols and motifs into his designs to evoke a sense of otherworldly allure. To this day, the brand's connection to the mysterious and the magical remains intact.

COLOUR ALCHEMY
TAPPING INTO ITS POWER

When you reach for the clothes in your wardrobe you may not fully recognize the science, psychology, cultural references or the healing properties you are gravitating towards.

Colour has the power to influence your emotions and behaviours. Interior designers, schools and hospitals utilize colour strategically; cool colours are often used to create calming environments, while warm colours are used to energize and invigorate.

The link between colour and emotion is partly due to cultural associations, and partly due to how our brains are wired to respond to different colours in specific ways. For instance, the colour red can trigger increased adrenaline production, leading to heightened emotions and elevated energy levels. This physiological response is why marketers and designers have strategically used the psychology of colour to influence specific emotions or behaviours. Colours are chosen deliberately to influence your mood and decision-making: red is used to inspire urgency, blue to evoke calm, green to indicate health.

Historically, colours have been used by tribes and ancient civilizations. For instance, the ancient Egyptians used colour in their art and rituals to symbolize deities: blue was associated with the god Amun and represented sky and water, green symbolized fertility and rebirth and was often linked to the god Osiris, red represented chaos and destruction as well as victory and was associated with Sekhmet, and gold symbolized the divine and the gods' immortality.

Now, let's break down the science of how we see colour.

There is a dance of energy that constantly circulates us, including various energy waves that are part of an electromagnetic spectrum. Some of this energy is invisible to us, such as microwaves, Wi-Fi, Bluetooth, radio waves from our mobile phones, and the infrared on our remote controls. Visible energy waves, known as visible light, are part of the visible spectrum. These light waves we can see have different lengths, which we perceive as different colours.

Each wavelength corresponds to a specific colour: red has the longest wavelength, while blue and violet have the shortest wavelengths. Think of a rainbow, it is a perfect example of this spectrum of visible light. The outermost colour, red, represents the longest wavelength, while the innermost colour, violet, represents the shortest. When you see different colours, you're actually seeing light waves of various lengths. Our eyes detect these light waves, and depending on the wavelength, we perceive different colours. The colour we see also depends on how the visible light interacts with objects – whether it's absorbed, reflected, or refracted.

Our mind, body and soul receive and interpret the energy waves of colour, which can trigger biochemical reactions in the body influencing physical health such as blood pressure, hormone levels and heart rate. Additionally, colour has the profound ability to evoke emotions that shift your mood. Yet, the power of colour goes further than its immediate effects on physical and emotional states. There are cultural, historical and scientific contexts. By understanding and harnessing the colour spectrum, we can unlock its transformative potential and integrate it into our lives, enhancing both our well-being and our connection to the world around us.

THE CHANEL COLOUR WHEEL
DECODING HER SIGNATURE PALETTE

The Chanel uniform delivers a colour palette that is as effortless as it is chic. By using these dress codes, you can intentionally infuse your outfit with the energy you desire. The key to embodying your chosen energy aesthetic? It begins with this colour wheel – wear these colours and luxurious textures to consciously embody their energies.

✦ **BLACK:** Grounding, Clarity, Modernity, Protection.

✦ **BLACK & WHITE:** Duality, Balance, Confidence, Order.

✦ **PEARLS:** Magical, Classic, Feminine.

✦ **TWEED:** Authoritative, Intelligent, Glamorous.

✦ **WHITE:** Light, Innocence, Purity, Dreamer, Clarity.

✦ **BEIGE:** Neutral, Simple, Sophisticated, Minimal, Understated.

✦ **GOLD & METALLICS:** Life-giving, Energizing, Abundance.

✦ **PASTELS:** Playful, Youthful, Optimistic.

✦ **NAVY:** Mystical, Deep, Focused.

✦ **RED:** Bold, Brave, Romantic, Audacious.

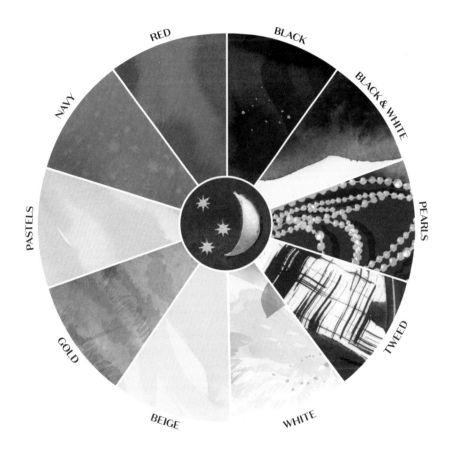

RED

BLACK

BLACK & WHITE

NAVY

PEARLS

PASTELS

TWEED

GOLD

WHITE

BEIGE

UNLOCKING THE ORACLE

A GUIDE TO USING THIS BOOK

As you work with this book to discover your ideal sartorial energy solution know that the answers you land on aren't driven by random chance – this Fashion Oracle offers a divination practice that invites synchronicity and intuition to reveal meaningful guidance and messages from a higher source. Influenced by the spirit of Chanel, it serves as a manual for dressing in harmony with the energy you wish to manifest. By blending fashion intuition with universal energies, this book offers clarity to help you navigate your wardrobe choices with purpose and insight.

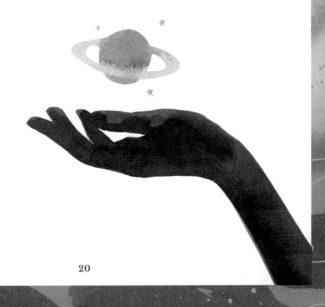

How it works:

1

✦ **INTENTION:** Clearly focus on a fashion question for which you wish to seek guidance. This intention directs your energy towards finding an answer to your fashion conundrum.

✦ **INTUITION:** Flick through the pages of this book, first turning the pages backwards to the left and then forwards to the right. As you gently fan through the pages, your fingertips may pause or feel drawn to a particular page and archetype.

2

3

✦ **SYNCHRONICITY:** The page you land on will reveal words, phrases or symbols that offer insights to guide your fashion choices.

ARCHETYPES EXPLAINED

THEIR ROLE IN MYTH AND PSYCHOLOGY

Think of an archetype as a universal template representing shared human experiences and emotions. Archetypes provide insights into human behaviour and the unconscious mind and have historically been used to help navigate life's challenges.

The term "archetype" was popularized by Carl Jung, who identified four major archetypes that offer a framework for understanding the dynamics present in human experience and storytelling. Jung's work explored the deeper layers of the psyche and the collective unconscious shared by humanity. The concept of archetypes has been adopted by various disciplines including literature, mythology and modern psychology. Archetypes also feature prominently in tarot, particularly in the Major Arcana, which represents key archetypal figures and themes.

For the purpose of this book, connecting with these archetypes will give you valuable guidance on your fashion dilemmas through their symbolic forms, profound meanings, and their insights into the human psyche. Should you choose to listen to their guidance you can connect with the aspects they hold within you, as they guide you to the answers to your innermost fashion desires and questions.

1

REBEL WITH A CAUSE

When the world you wish to be a part of doesn't exist, it is you who must establish a new normal. The archetypes in this chapter will offer you the strength and resilience to reject the status quo and current patterns of conformity, as they invite you to mix audacity with a style that is both daring and sophisticated.

To dress as a rebel (*with* a cause) is to defy conventional fashion norms and showcase a strong, unapologetic sense of self as you embrace your inner spirit of defiance and nonconformity.

★

"A GIRL SHOULD BE TWO THINGS: WHO AND WHAT SHE WANTS."

Coco Chanel

THE REBEL

EMBRACE THE TRANSFORMATIVE POWER OF THE TROUSER.

D on the fabric of defiance by embracing the legacy of liberation in the form of trousers, for in their folds lies the spirit of revolution. Let the trouser speak to your non-conformist attitude needed for the tasks of the day as you stride boldly into the realm where power and poise intertwine. Hear the echo of Coco Chanel's fearless whisper guiding you to take your own path, regardless of the societal norms and expectations that surround you.

*

Wearing a pair of trousers was one of Coco's first rebellions. Her commitment to challenging gender stereotypes of the time transformed trousers into a symbol of liberation and modernity, rejecting the constrictive and impractical fashions that were otherwise the norm for women. Coco borrowed trousers from the boys and never gave them back – they became a permanent staple in her collections, embodying freedom, progress, and the modern woman. Trousers allowed the wearer to move freely and adapt to changing attitudes in the workforce of the era.

Repeat these words, and have them become your mantra:
"I am one, but my rebellious act, whether big or small,
has the power to unite many and spark a movement.
As I stand for change, others will follow. Together, we
have the strength to revolutionize."

THE REVOLUTIONARY

DON'T SACRIFICE COMFORT FOR STYLE – OPT FOR COMFORTABLE MATERIALS THAT LET YOU MOVE.

Embrace the Revolutionary archetype's spirit of change and transformation. Coco Chanel revolutionized women's fashion by introducing practical yet elegant designs that departed from the restrictive and ornate styles of the early twentieth century. Her use of jersey fabric, relaxed silhouettes and menswear-inspired elements challenged conventional notions of femininity and paved the way for more comfortable and functional clothing for women.

Coco's vision extended beyond the physical aspects of fashion. Her designs encouraged women to take up space, to move with confidence, and to reject the antiquated notions of beauty that had long confined them. She once famously said, "Luxury must be comfortable, otherwise it is not luxury." This ethos permeated every piece she created, redefining luxury to include comfort and empowerment.

An affirmation to revolutionize change: "I hold the courage and conviction to challenge the old and embrace the new. I am a catalyst for change and my actions ignite transformation."

THE RISK-TAKER

LET YOUR ACCESSORIES SERVE AS EXCLAMATION POINTS TO AMPLIFY YOUR BOLDNESS AND INDIVIDUALITY.

True risk-taking lies not in following trends but in forging your own path with courage and conviction. It is about pushing boundaries, defying expectations, and fearlessly expressing your unique point of view and identity through fashion. Command attention by adding drama and intrigue to your look with accessories that serve as a statement to instantly transform an outfit.

*

In the ever-evolving landscape of fashion, Coco Chanel stands as the quintessence of audacity and elegance – she was unafraid to take risks and redefine the essence of style. Coco's risk-taking ethos was about challenging the boundaries and norms that confine you, and reimagining luxury for the modern age.

Journalling prompt: "In what areas of my life am I holding back and playing safe? In what areas of my life could I be pushing boundaries?"

Trust in your instincts and boldly pursue your passions, for in the dance with uncertainty, your greatest potential is revealed.

THE FEMINIST

A NEW SILHOUETTE.

R ecognize your beauty and celebrate your curves and contours, for your body is the vessel that holds your unique spirit. Embrace your silhouette and build a deep, loving relationship with your body by honouring its natural form. Rather than distorting your body into society's shape of beauty, appreciate your body, focusing on the joy it brings into your life.

*

Coco Chanel's audacious spirit and pioneering vision not only redefined women's fashion but also contributed significantly to the empowerment of women in the early twentieth century. Her legacy lies in the profound cultural shift she inspired. In 1910, Coco defiantly rejected the corset and changed the course of fashion forever. By removing the corset, she not only altered the silhouette of fashion but also challenged the societal expectations placed on women and provided a new template for femininity – one that was strong, independent and unapologetically free.

By being one of the first couturiers to replace boned corsets with soft, flowing fabrics, Coco empowered women to embrace their natural shapes and live life with a new-found sense of autonomy. The removal of the corset was nothing short of a sartorial revolution.

Guidance: Cultivate gratitude for your body and all it does for you. Place your hands tenderly on the parts of your body you normally conceal, give it thanks and send it unconditional love. Connect with and honour your body, for it is the home that carries you through life's journey.

THE INDIVIDUALIST

BEHOLD THE REALM OF ANDROGYNOUS ATTIRE, WHERE NONCONFORMITY REIGNS SUPREME.

The Individualist archetype values personal freedom, defining its identity outside societal norms and expectations. Connect to your true self and style regardless of the herd that surrounds you. Harness your personal style by elevating your personal identity, and let your outfit be the vehicle to express it. Embrace gender fluidity in your ensemble, allowing ancient binaries of gender to dissolve into the ether.

*

Coco Chanel's embrace of androgynous style stands out as a testament to her fearless innovation. She dared to defy convention and introduced simplicity, comfort and a sense of freedom to her clothes. Coco defied the fashion norms around gender – one notable instance occurred at the races in the early 1920s, where she famously wore a masculine-inspired outfit in a sea of women traditionally dressed in dresses and hats. Coco's decision to wear trousers at the races made a powerful statement about women's fashion and autonomy which challenged and redefined the very essence of femininity. It contributed to the gradual acceptance of trousers as appropriate attire for women, paving the way for future generations to embrace androgynous styles and more practical clothing options without sacrificing on glamour and style.

Guidance: Dare to challenge binary thinking around gender. Whether it comes from within you or from the world around you, reflect on gender-based assumptions that you hold or you have been conditioned to accept.

THE RULE-BREAKER

AS YOU JOURNEY THROUGH THE WAKING WORLD, DRESS IN PYJAMA-INSPIRED ELEGANCE.

The Rule-Breaker archetype represents a spirit of defiance and innovation, unafraid to challenge conventions and redefine what is to be expected. This archetype thrives on the audacity to disrupt established norms, paving the way for new expressions of identity and style.

Embody a spirit of effortless confidence and timeless allure as you blur the lines between night and day with grace and sophistication. Coco Chanel broke many fashion rules, bucking traditional dressing and current silhouettes of the era while never compromising on elegance. There is an allure to pyjama dressing and an indulgence in taking an outfit typically reserved for the comfort of your bed and seamlessly blending the realms of loungewear with haute couture. It takes a level of sophistication to effortlessly redefine rigid dress codes and embrace a new paradigm of chic allure. Pyjama dressing becomes not just a fashion statement but a manifesto of liberation, a testament to the enduring power of sartorial subversion and where pyjamas become not just an ensemble you have put together but an ethos.

An affirmation to support realignment: "I possess the courage to chart my own course, undeterred or distracted by the societal norms that surround me."

If the rules you live by are outdated and challenge reason, embody the bravery to defy norms and forge your own path.

THE ALCHEMIST

TRANSMUTE YOUR ENERGY FROM ONE VIBRATION TO ANOTHER THROUGH THE POWER OF MONOTONE.

W/earing black and white together harmonizes your outfit by balancing the energies of opposites – yin and yang, good and evil, life and death. The high-contrast duality of a black and white colour palette reflects a state of equilibrium, bringing harmony and alchemy to your look.

*

Coco Chanel understood the art of alchemizing her past pain into a compelling future through her career. The challenges she faced in her past can be seen directly in her designs. The colour palette of black and white synonymous with Chanel has been said to be inspired by the nuns' uniforms from her childhood. And her famous string of pearls? Echoes from the nuns' rosary beads.

In the ever-evolving world of fashion where trends come and go, Coco's black and white creations remain a steadfast beacon of style. They remind us that true elegance lies in simplicity. Coco's mastery of the black and white palette continues to influence designers and fashion houses worldwide. The understated glamour of this colour combination remains a celebrated fashion pillar.

Guidance: Are you able to be at peace and totally in love with both the light and the dark aspects that you hold? Integrate the dark (your shadow self) by bringing to light the unconscious or repressed emotions and behaviours you hold. With patience, compassion, and love, embrace these hidden parts of you. As you learn to accept your shadow you fall in love with the totality of who you are – warts and all.

THE DEBATER

USE YOUR CLOTHES AS A MEANS TO SPARK CONVERSATION AND INSPIRE DIALOGUE.

A shirt calls to you – a symbol of structure and clarity. Whether tailored, oversized or cropped, embrace the comfort of its crisp lines to exude confidence and authority when presenting your arguments. The Debater archetype thrives on dialogue, challenge and the exploration of different perspectives. Wearing a shirt will assert your presence with an air of understated sophistication. Elevate this look further with a touch of sparkle and jewels, infusing a touch of feminine elegance.

*

Use your clothes as a means to foster debate. Coco Chanel, the ultimate fashion disruptor, sparked a debate on how women should dress. She famously challenged societal norms of her era by popularizing black as an everyday colour instead of one traditionally reserved for mourning or uniforms. She also blurred the lines between masculine and feminine dressing, creating men's shirts for women that were often paired with a tie or cravat, bringing androgyny to the forefront of her designs.

Guidance: Mastering the art of listening is essential to becoming a skilled debater. Discerning the cadence of speech and silence is key to navigating discussions effectively.

THE COMET

LEAVE A SPARKLING TRAIL OF LIGHT IN YOUR WAKE WITH YOUR EVERY STEP.

Whether embroidered onto garments or crafted into accessories, add a touch of celestial beauty to your outfit. Shooting through the pitch-black cosmos, comets leave a trail of ice-like dust and gas which extends for millions of kilometres, illuminated by stars as they voyage through space. These rebellious and dramatic celestial bodies undergo a profound transformation as they approach the sun. When looking at the arc of a comet's journey across the sky it symbolizes themes of dramatic change, transformation, unpredictability and exploration throughout their passage through the solar system.

*

Their celestial allure and symbolism of destiny, aspiration and the infinite possibilities of the universe appealed to Coco Chanel. It is no wonder she found inspiration in these symbols – stars and celestial forms are recurring motifs in the designs at Chanel.

Coco's love for comets can clearly be seen in her 1932 collection Bijoux de Diamants, which embraced celestial themes. Among these pieces the Comète diamond necklace stood out: its diamonds arranged in a stunning display that showed off the beauty of these cosmic travellers with their shimmering tails. These pieces were more than accessories; they were statements of radiant confidence and aspirational beauty.

Guidance: As you embrace the aspects of the comet within you, recognize that while your path may be solitary, your impact is boundless. Journey through life with a fearless spirit, knowing that transformation is your destiny.

THE ACTIVIST

MERGE THE STRENGTH OF MASCULINE CODES IN YOUR BASE LAYERS WITH A FEMININE FINISH.

Balance the energies in today's ensemble by complementing the masculine elements of your look with pearls or a silk scarf to achieve sartorial harmony. Embrace the strength of unity; it's in the coexistence of contrasts that a truly harmonious whole is formed.

*

Coco Chanel brilliantly captured this concept, styling both male and female models in her campaigns in identical clothing. The only distinction? Pearls and a camellia-adorned headband for the female model. This mirrored reflection was Coco's bold statement on gender equality.

The Activist archetype sees more than the surface of what is but the potential of what could be. They are the bridge between the present and the future. Their presence stirs the hearts of others, inspiring collective movements towards a more just and equitable reality. Coco wasn't shouting in the streets with a placard, but she was deeply passionate about making great changes. Her cause was women, and her conduit was fashion. Coco gave women clothes that offered comfort and ease normally reserved for the wardrobes of men. We take so much for granted for what women now find in their wardrobes, but it took radical thinking and action, and Coco delivered it with fashion flair.

Reflection: The wounded feminine asks: "Am I too much?" In contrast, the wounded masculine asks: "Am I enough?" We all hold aspects of both the masculine and feminine within us. Get curious where your wounded feminine shrinks in life and where your wounded masculine takes up excessive space.

THE DREAMER

MANIFEST YOUR DREAMS WITH THE POWER OF LAYERED JEWELLERY, ACTING AS A TALISMAN FOR INSPIRATION AND MAGIC.

Our dreams are the genesis of creation. They don't play by the rules of 3D logic and what may have previously existed – they serve as our compass to expand into new realities. When we connect with our dreams, our body intuitively responds and we begin the process of grounding those visions from the 4th dimension (your dream state) into the 3rd dimension (the tangible world of our waking life). Hold or wear a talisman to help create a mental and emotional connection to your dreams and desired outcomes.

*

Karl Lagerfeld understood the power of connecting to dreams and it is said that he claimed many of his ideas came from his dreams. It is believed he once said: "The best things I've ever done have come from my dreams. Sometimes, it's the whole show, including the sets. I dreamed it all."

Dream journal: Connect with your dreams via a dream journal. Upon waking, immediately record the fragments and feelings of your dreams. This practice will bridge your dream realm with your waking life, revealing the insights and guidance hidden within. As you consistently strengthen this connection, the universe will recognize this channel as a means to communicate with you more frequently via the astral realm.

THE IDEALIST

IN THE STILLNESS OF COMFORT YOUR TRUE ESSENCE EMERGES, UNBURDENED BY THE DISTRACTIONS OF DISCOMFORT.

To connect with the importance of comfort, begin by honouring your body's need for ease and tranquillity. Let comfort guide your choices, for when you are at ease, your mind and spirit can soar freely. Embrace the softness, the warmth and the serenity that a comfortable outfit offers, for it is in these moments that you align with your deepest self and the greater harmony of the universe.

*

Coco Chanel opted for comfortable fabrics and silhouettes using fluid fabrics like jersey and tweed that allowed for ease of movement. By rejecting the restrictive corsets and stiff fabrics of her time, and emphasizing comfort, Coco symbolized a rejection of outdated norms and a celebration of women's freedom and autonomy.

Coco's idealism was deeply rooted in her desire to liberate women through fashion. This was her commitment to creating positive change in the world. Individuals who resonate with the Idealist archetype are often guided by higher principles, values and a vision of a more harmonious and enlightened society. Coco designed clothes for the world she envisioned and for the woman she was within that world.

Guidance: Evolving often involves eliminating. Let go of life's burdens that have weighed you down for far too long. By releasing outdated identities, people, behaviours and thought patterns, you make space for new opportunities. Sometimes, you don't feel the weight of something until you let it go.

THE MODERN WOMAN

ALL HAIL THE LITTLE BLACK DRESS.

The Modern Woman is multifaceted; while staying true to her values and ambitions, she navigates a complex world with resilience, creativity and an ability to adapt to changing times.

*

Introduced in 1926 the little black dress, or the LBD, designed by Coco Chanel is arguably one of the most utilized and relied-upon fashion pieces in history. Before Chanel, black was reserved for mourning or the uniform of a maid; it was sombre, severe and far from chic. But Coco, with her innate understanding of sophistication and modernity, transformed black into the epitome of effortless style and luxurious glamour. Turning luxury on its head, she altered the energy of the colour black and redefined understated elegance.

Connect to the archetype of the Modern Woman by wearing a hard-working LBD for either daytime or evening dressing. Its deceptive simplicity exudes confidence, and a century after its conception, this go-to for every occasion is still worn by countless women and remains a staple in every modern fashion wardrobe. An easy win to signal power, elegance and authority, the LBD is the ultimate equalizer, making high fashion accessible to all women, regardless of their status.

Guidance: As you navigate life's changing chapters, honour your intuition as much as your intellect, and let the wisdom of your heart guide your decisions as much as your mind. Engage with the world around you, but never lose sight of your inner world as you continue to evolve and transform.

THE INDEPENDENT WOMAN

NEVER OVERLOOK THE POWER OF A FUNCTIONAL POCKET POSITIONED *JUST SO.*

B lend elegance with purpose and prioritize outfits with pockets, belts and adjustable closures. These utilitarian details support the Independent archetype's qualities of self-sufficiency while combining beauty with practicality, allowing every piece you wear to serve both your aesthetic and functional needs.

*

For Coco Chanel, pockets are not just an afterthought – they were a statement that sat with intent and were often complete with the iconic double C logo or a subtle trim. Pockets follow the Chanel ethos that beauty will also serve a purpose.

No button was stitched without a buttonhole, and no pocket was designed to be merely decorative. Coco's clothes resonated with independent, resilient and modern women worldwide. To this day, if you compliment a woman on her outfit, she will often exclaim: *"And* it has pockets!"

To the untrained eye, a pocket may seem purely functional, a small, inconsequential space to hold your lipstick or slip in your hand. But in the world of Chanel, the pocket is power, history and style – all sewn into a single seam.

Guidance: Prioritize self-care. Without tending to your own needs, even the most resilient can feel the weight of their responsibilities. By taking care of yourself, you reinforce a deep self-trust that your energy will always be preserved. This trust empowers you to take on more opportunities with confidence, *free from the fear of burnout, knowing that your well-being is safeguarded and your capacity to handle more is enhanced.*

2

BOSS MODE

This chapter is for those who have a
readiness to lead, take decisive action and
hustle. The archetypes within this chapter
offer guidance to align with your North Star
and mission, empowering you to lead with
clarity, intent and unwavering purpose.

"DON'T SPEND TIME BEATING ON A WALL, HOPING TO TRANSFORM IT INTO A DOOR."

Coco Chanel

THE BOSS

ALIGN YOUR OUTER APPEARANCE AND YOUR INNER AMBITIONS WITH CLEAN STRUCTURED LINES AND SHARP, PURPOSEFUL SOPHISTICATION.

Are you ready for your boss mode to be activated? Command attention in any meeting with a classic suit – choose a boxy silhouette to bring focused clarity to your energy. This outfit balances your feminine power with your masculine drive.

*

Coco Chanel was a figure of profound complexity. Unapologetically ruthless, Coco had a sharp business acumen that allowed her to outmanoeuvre her male counterparts. She was fiercely competitive, evident in her controversial tactics as she used every advantage to protect and advance her brand. Most shockingly and as is now widely known, during the Second World War Coco fought to regain control of her fragrance line from her Jewish partners by attempting to exploit the Vichy government's anti-Semitic laws, and took advantage of her connections with Nazi officials. Take heed of the still ongoing debate around Coco's personal moral compass – when you choose the type of boss you want to be, the pursuit of success and personal gain above all else could compromise you.

Guidance: Declare authority and project self-assurance in any setting by adhering to these tenets:
1. Sit or stand tall. This posture opens up your body, an easy win to project confidence.
2. Hold good eye contact.
3. Monitor your internal dialogue and replace negative thinking with positive thoughts. In life, you may find yourself entering a room of bullies. Make sure that your mind isn't one of them.

THE WARRIOR

CHOOSE AN ARMOUR WITH METALLIC ACCENTS SUCH AS CHAINS AND ZIPPERS THAT GIVE A MASCULINE MILITARY EDGE.

U nfazed by obstacles, the Warrior archetype represents the inner drive to protect, defend, and overcome adversity, often linked to themes of self-discipline, bravery, and perseverance. Their energy is assertive and commanding yet grounded in a sense of purpose, whether it's fighting for personal boundaries, advocating for others, or breaking down barriers in pursuit of change.

*

Coco Chanel frequently explored the balance of masculine and feminine duality in her designs – masterfully juxtaposing hardware against feminine details and materials, creating a signature style that exudes both strength and elegance. Her innovative use of chains, buttons and metallic accents contrasted beautifully with soft tweeds, delicate silks and intricate lace. This bold combination not only defined Chanel's aesthetic but also offered a modern take on femininity that remains timeless and influential. Whether through the iconic chain-link straps of her quilted bags, belts and accessories or the bold, structured buttons on her classic tweed jackets, Chanel's designs seamlessly blend masculine and feminine features. Creating pieces that are both powerful and graceful, they give the wearer a coat of arms that is equally balanced in the divine masculine and feminine energies.

Affirmation: "Give me clarity and reveal truths that I need to cut away from my life." Connect to your sword of truth by visualizing yourself wielding a radiant sword that cuts through illusions and falsehoods.

THE ENTREPRENEUR

GO BEYOND CLOTHING AND OPT FOR AN INVISIBLE ACCESSORY. COMPLETE YOUR LOOK WITH A SIGNATURE SCENT.

Today, as you stand at the crossroads of choice, embrace the power of transformation in the seemingly simple change of your scent.

*

When Chanel Nº5 debuted in 1921, its bottle design and minimal packaging were groundbreaking. The rectangular, crystal-clear bottle with sharp angles was a departure from the ornate vessels of the era. By showing off the golden liquid inside, Coco made the scent itself the focus. The minimal packaging, featuring only the brand name on a plain label (which ingeniously needed no translation into other languages), challenged the era's norms of opulence.

The number five holds a deep, almost mystical significance in the world of Chanel. Chanel Nº5 was the fifth scent chosen from samples provided. The stars aligned with this choice, as Coco's rising sun was in Leo, the fifth sign of the zodiac. Adding to the allure, it is fabled that the perfume was launched on May 5th (the fifth day of the fifth month). For Coco, the number 5 wasn't just a number; it was a symbol of her destiny, becoming a recurring motif woven into Chanel's legacy.

Coco understood her customers – their needs, preferences and pain points. Her customer-centric approach led her to design a perfume that "smelled like a woman" rather than a flower, offering a tribute to the modern woman who dared to redefine beauty.

Guidance: As you anoint yourself with your favourite potion, boldly envision the "you" you aspire to be emerging as your skin takes on this new fragrance.

THE MERMAID

ADORN YOURSELF WITH THE TREASURES OF THE SEA IN SHIMMERING PEARLS.

The Mermaid holds an ability to communicate through song and uses her enchanting voice to mesmerize and hypnotize others with her irresistible allure. Coco Chanel knew the secrets of the mermaid and wielded her voice to transform the fashion world. Her words spoke creations into existence, while her charm captivated those around her.

*

Coco famously wore strings of cascading pearls – they became her signature look, a style said to be initially gifted to her by an early lover, Étienne Balsan. Coco cherished pearls for their symbolism of femininity and the purity associated with them, and wore them to celebrate the strength, resilience and beauty inherent in women. Her affinity for pearls may also stem from their formation within the depths of the ocean, reflecting a journey of transformation and growth akin to the personal development and wisdom gained through life experiences. Coco revolutionized the perception of pearls in fashion, elevating them from traditional and conservative to symbols of modernity, luxury and empowerment.

Guidance: Recognize the power of your voice and understand that each utterance spoken must carry purpose. Harness the resonance of your frequency to ignite influence, and speak only truths you are prepared to manifest. For your words shape the reality that surrounds you.

THE SELF-STARTER

WITH EACH TILT, AND WITH EACH ANGLE, YOUR HAT WILL ADD A NARRATIVE TO ANY ENSEMBLE.

Coco Chanel's rags-to-riches journey as an orphan girl who turned herself into one of the wealthiest women of her time begins in the world of millinery. Coco first embarked into the world of entrepreneurship in the early twentieth century, establishing herself as a force of creativity and business acumen by designing and selling hats. This not only showcased her innate talent for business but also marked the genesis of her iconic style philosophy – minimal, sophisticated, and timeless yet modern. Gone were the ostentatious plumes and elaborate embellishments of the past; in their place, Coco introduced clean lines, luxurious fabrics and understated details that emphasized comfort and effortless style. Her visionary approach to design and business laid the foundation for a global empire.

The choice of wearing a hat isn't necessarily a practical choice against the weather. View the hat as a protective shield for your energy, keeping you grounded and centred while you navigate your daily life. The ritualistic gesture of donning a hat is akin to placing a crown upon your head. Treat this action with mindful respect as you connect to your crown chakra – an energy centre located just above the head associated with higher consciousness and spiritual connection.

When placing a hat on your head, do so with intent and repeat this affirmation: "I am connected to my higher self and open to the divine guidance that supports my highest timeline." The crown chakra serves as a gateway to your higher consciousness and spiritual enlightenment.

THE SUN

LET GOLDEN SUNSHINE LIFE-GIVING HUES DRAPE YOUR FORM, FOR IN ITS EMBRACE LIES THE POWER OF RENEWAL AND VITALITY.

By connecting with the Sun archetype, you tap into the power to sustain life and illuminate the world around you – as you wear this attire, you will embody the sun's life-giving energy and infuse your aura with a vibrant *joie de vivre*. These colours and luminous fabrics will make you feel invigorated and truly alive.

As you hold this energy, you will find that many gravitate towards you and eagerly bask in your warmth, benefiting from the presence of your golden rays. Don't conceal your light – let it shine bright. Allow yourself to shine without reservation, your presence brightens every room you enter as you cast beams of light with your every move.

*

Both the sun and Coco Chanel hold iconic status as they share qualities of brilliance, influence and longevity. During her career, Coco gravitated towards metallic fabrics for her evening wear, alongside pioneering textiles that replicate the luminosity of precious metals. These fabrics impart a delicate sun-like shimmer to the garment's surface.

Meditation: Focus on what you wish to bring to life. As you hold this intention, visualize yourself breathing in golden light with every inhale. With each breath, feel these golden rays permeate your being, illuminating every cell with life-affirming luminosity that will give life to your goals.

THE PIONEER

FINISH YOUR LOOK WITH A PUSSYCAT BOW, MERGING SOFT ALLURE WITH COMMANDING PRESENCE.

Wearing a pussycat bow is a fashion choic that is both symbolic and strategic. It blends tradition with elegance, demonstrating that femininity and power are not mutually exclusive. Pairing a billowing pussycat bow with today's look projects a new kind of authority – one that embraces both strength and grace as you conquer new frontiers.

*

At Chanel, Coco Chanel and Karl Lagerfeld redefined style, each pioneering a new vision of luxury for their respective eras. Encouraged by the Pioneer archetype, you are opening the door for others. It's more than you – it is a movement that extends beyond yourself. The responsibility of exploring new frontiers can sometimes lead to feelings of isolation or detachment from those who do not share the same vision. To stay grounded, connect with other visionaries and pioneers who share your beliefs and goals. A supportive network can reinforce the belief that visions are precursors to reality.

Visualization: If you can see it, it's already on its way – it just hasn't arrived yet. Regularly practise visualization techniques by vividly imagining your future successes in detail. As you rewire your mind you'll come to realize that your visions are glimpses of what is to come.

THE VISIONARY

TO TRULY SEE BEYOND LIFE'S ILLUSIONS, BEGIN BY EMBRACING THEM IN YOUR WARDROBE.

I ncorporate pieces that play with perception, such as a dropped waist, to symbolize your ability to discern deeper truths. By weaving these illusions into your style, you embody the wisdom to unveil the illusions that cloud your vision. Coco Chanel envisioned a future where women stood on the same platform as men. She wanted independence for women, she wanted financial freedom for women, she wanted liberation for women. Dress for the future you desire; dress as the man, the woman, or the them that you are aspiring to step into, aligning your style with a future you want to create.

*

Masculine dropped waists and simple silhouettes with heavy materials blurred the lines between masculine and feminine dressing as Coco experimented with silhouettes, textures and proportions.

Affirmation: "I ignite self-transformation and lead with visionary strength."
Do you see who you are? Or do you see yourself only in relation to others? Your identity isn't shaped by your environment or relationships, but by your unique journey, choices and inner world. Allow yourself the freedom to define who you are on your own terms, independent of the illusions and expectations placed on you. Embrace the process of truly seeing yourself by stepping out of your usual environments and exploring new experiences. Challenge yourself to step out of your comfort zone and strengthen your connection to your inner compass as a trusted tool to navigate these experiences. In doing so, you will see that the need to seek external validation is released.

"FASHION ALCHEMY IS THE ART OF CHANGING YOUR ENERGY VIA THE CLOTHES YOU WEAR."

THE COUTURIÈRE

EMBRACE THE PRECISION OF SHARP TAILORING TO UNLOCK CONCENTRATED POWER AND INNER MASTERY.

A teacher of style, Coco Chanel has taught us how to dress since the early 1910s – an unquestionable authority on dressing for women. Lean into Coco's precision for detail and opt for sharp tailoring. Look for structured silhouettes, clean lines and a precise cut.

*

A renowned couturière, Coco was celebrated for her meticulous attention to detail which set her apart in the world of fashion. Coco's reputation as a couturière was built upon her unwavering commitment to precision and detail, and her belief in the importance of tailoring and fit. She crafted her designs to flatter the female form, paying close attention to how each piece draped and moved on the body – often pinning garments directly onto her models. This was a lengthy but dedicated process which ensured that her clients not only looked stylish but also felt comfortable in her clothes.

Let each stitch and detail of your outfit reflect a dedication to timeless elegance and craftsmanship. Trust in your intuition to weave together a look centred around fabric and form.

Affirmation: "I channel both creativity and precision to transform ideas into reality. These intertwined forces bring balance to my focus, visions and purpose as I bring them to life with flawless execution."

THE BUSINESSWOMAN

A WARDROBE HERO CAN DO A LOT OF HEAVY LIFTING TO TRANSLATE YOUR PERSONAL STYLE TO THE WORLD.

B e it your bag, shoes or statement jacket, the right hero piece allows you to move through the world with a balance of confidence and grace.

*

Coco Chanel understood the power of a strong brand and used herself as a living mannequin to signify what it meant to be a modern woman. Develop your personal brand alongside your style by investing in a wardrobe hero. It doesn't have to be expensive. Plus the added value comes from wearing it repeatedly to reduce the cost per wear. This isn't about covering yourself in logos either. It's about expressing to the world who you are through well-chosen, hard-working fashion staples.

The Chanel 2.55 designer handbag became a status symbol, named after the month and year in which it was launched, February 1955. The design was born from a desire for simplicity and practicality – when evening bags of that era were traditionally a clutch, Coco added a shoulder strap, plus interior pockets (including a specific pocket to hold lipstick) to support everyday functionality. When Karl Lagerfeld joined Chanel in 1983, he introduced the now-iconic interlocking CC logo to the bag's design, which replaced the original "Mademoiselle" twist lock, giving the 2.55 a modernized look while still honouring its timeless design.

Guidance: As you navigate a roadmap of aligned goals, know that a past version of you is so proud of how far you have come, and a future you is so very grateful for all the hard work you have put in.

THE TRAILBLAZER

OPT FOR THE GENTLE LINES OF SOFT TAILORING TODAY. THEY WILL GUIDE YOU TO MOVE WITH A QUIET STRENGTH AND CONFIDENCE.

There is a softness you can lean into when you lead. It doesn't need to be all gritted teeth and a *charge forward* mentality. The ability to stay soft in moments of action offers you the clarity to see the path ahead of you with complete clarity and a quiet, knowing confidence in your choices. It is a paradox of immense strength to remain soft when faced with challenges that require decisive action. Only the truly powerful can wield gentleness amid the complexities of leadership.

*

Draw inspiration from the creative path Coco Chanel forged by opting for tailoring that has a relaxed fit and a softer silhouette when choosing your garments – it will gift you the harmonious union of strength and gentleness as you fuse masculine-inspired tailoring with feminine elegance.

Affirmation: "There is strength in my softness."

Trust in your ability to lead with authenticity and inspire others to do the same along the way. Remember, the Trailblazer paves the road for change and leaves a legacy of boldness and determination.

THE MESSENGER

CHOOSE AN ATTIRE THAT DANCES WITH YOUR EVERY MOVEMENT.

Embrace embellishments such as sequins, or opt for silhouettes that effortlessly follow your lead. The Messenger archetype is a vessel for divine communication – a conduit through which truth flows, and connections are forged across realms. Dressing to convey an important message with style and impact requires a blend of fashion-forward thinking, practicality and a sense of forward movement. Embrace embellishments such as sequins, or opt for silhouettes that effortlessly follow your lead.

*

Coco Chanel used techniques that imbued her garments with a dynamic sense of movement and fluidity, such as using sequins to create wave-like patterns. The sequinned waves produce a mesmerizing visual effect, causing the garment to appear to ripple and shimmer as the wearer moves – a striking effect and especially captivating if you plan to share your message under the spotlight. Coco's message to the world transcends mere style; she communicated themes of empowerment, elegance and radical independence. Her messages revolutionized fashion as we know it.

Before sharing your message, consider these codes of truth often linked to Socrates:

Is it true?
Is it kind?
Is it necessary?

A truth-teller must present the facts. By adhering to these principles, a Messenger can ensure that their message is delivered with integrity, clarity and a positive impact.

THE PHOENIX

FLY HIGH WITH FEATHER DETAILS – WHETHER A PRINTED PATTERN OR A BOLD, FEATHERY FRINGE.

As you dress today, let each garment ignite your inner flame. Pain often drives our personal evolution. The universe will often use discomfort to prompt change since comfort can lack the motivation to evolve. If you're in a "phoenix rising" moment – where everything seems to fall apart before a transformation – don't run from the pain. Avoiding it means avoiding your own evolution. Numbing the pain only delays your becoming. You need to feel it all and face it head-on, for the only way out is through. Endure the heat and you'll emerge stronger, having witnessed yourself walk through the flames. From the ashes of destruction a new phoenix rises, ready to soar higher. Through this process, you'll come to understand that there is nothing in life that can break you and nothing in life to fear.

*

Coco Chanel navigated many devastating metaphorical "fires" throughout her life. She grew up in poverty, suffered the loss of her great love in a car accident, and endured the arrest and detention of her nephew in a German prison camp during the Second World War. After the war she was exiled to Switzerland for her controversial involvement with a German officer – a period of her life that continues to cast a shadow over her legacy. There were many times when Coco was in the flames of life yet despite the pain she always got back up even stronger.

Guidance: Know that an ending is simply the start of a new beginning in disguise.

THE INNOVATOR

CONJURE VISIONS ANEW AND WEAVE DREAMS UNIMAGINED.

Consider how you can use pieces in your wardrobe in completely novel ways. Transcend the confines of the ordinary and eclipse the boundaries of the familiar as your attire becomes a canvas for experimentation and exploration. Fuelled by curiosity, embrace the Innovator archetype's spirit of ingenuity and creativity as you assemble your ensemble, daring to blend tradition with innovation and experiment with unconventional pairings. Delve into the depths of your wardrobe, uncovering treasures awaiting to be reborn in entirely new forms; a scarf braided into a necklace, an apron worn as a skirt, a belt transformed into a choker – all guided by the wisdom of your intuition and imagination.

*

Coco Chanel held a fashion lens that redefined norms. Her innate curiosity often led her to creative solutions, as she repurposed accessories and gave them a novel twist. She challenged assumptions and constantly thought outside the box. Taking a traditional brooch, typically designed to adorn the lapel of a blouse, Coco made it work harder by repurposing it on her hip or as a point of intrigue on her hat – an avant-garde and radical statement for the time.

Guidance: Spend today looking at everything in the world as if each moment is unfolding before your eyes for the very first time. Embrace a sense of curious wonder untethered from expectations and predictable outcomes.

THE SHAPE-SHIFTER

MATCH YOUR INNER REALITY WITH YOUR OUTER APPEARANCE WITH EXAGGERATED SILHOUETTES.

You have the choice to remain the same, or evolve. The Shape-shifter archetype embodies the ability to change form at will, reflecting the fluidity of identity and the ever-shifting nature of the self. When you adopt the energy of the Shape-shifter, you get to play with your identity, you have the power to shape-shift who you are, and translate your inner world into three-dimensional form. This power requires mastery. Don't use this gift merely to fit in, be wary of changing who you are to accommodate others. Instead, transcend your current form through the silhouette of your clothes to unlock limitless possibilities as you expand beyond the boundaries of your human vessel.

*

Karl Lagerfeld's tenure at Chanel was marked by his extraordinary ability to evolve and shape-shift the brand's identity, infusing the brand with a bold, modern edge while honouring its heritage. With his genius for reinvention, Lagerfeld played with proportions, pushing boundaries with oversized jackets, voluminous skirts and dramatic shoulders. These exaggerated forms were not mere fashion statements but a translation of his vision, turning garments into architectural wonders. Lagerfeld's shape-shifting designs for Chanel breathed new life into the brand, ensuring its continued evolution without losing the essence of Coco Chanel's original vision.

Before changing form, look within and ask yourself these questions:
1. Am I shape-shifting to make other people comfortable?
2. Am I holding back from the form I am meant to take?
3. What is the new shape I am ready to hold?

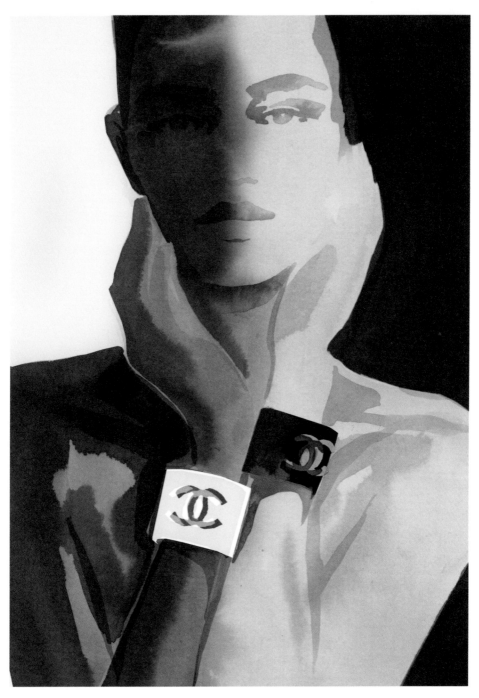

BALANCE

FIND SYMMETRY IN YOUR ENERGY BY BALANCING THE LIGHT AND THE DARK WITHIN.

Balance brings order to chaos. To harmonize the masculine and feminine energies within, consider the ancient symbols of power and grace – the cuff bracelets. A blend of strength and elegance, cuffs are more than mere adornments; they are symbols of authority and protection, and a cuff placed upon each wrist will invoke balance. Rooted in history, warriors and queens alike have worn cuffs to signify strength and resilience. Let the weight of the cuff be a reminder that you are grounded while they effortlessly elevate any ensemble.

*

Much like the detailing of a Chanel button, the Chanel cuff bracelets are characterized by their statement-making designs, blending materials such as leather, gold, enamel and pearls. They are often adorned with signature Chanel markings, including Coco's favourite camellia flower, a lion's head, or the interlocking CC logo – all of which contribute to their luxurious and dramatic aesthetic.

Breathwork: Balance isn't found, it is created. If you've been giving a lot of yourself, it's time to focus on receiving. To make a significant impact on the world and give (through your exhale), you must also be comfortable with receiving (via an equally substantial inhale).

Start with your breath. Place one hand on your heart and one hand on your belly. Inhale slowly for a count of eight. Pause. Exhale gently for a count of eight. Pause again. Gradually lengthen your breath, slowing down each count as you guide your mind and body into a harmonious flow of energy.

3

DIVINE FEMININE

As you embrace your divine feminine essence, you awaken an innate knowing – a sensual ability to be fully present in the moment, birthing ideas and nurturing future visions. The archetypes introduced in this chapter will help you tap into a deeper connection with your intuition, and embody a balanced expression of feminine energy in all aspects of life.

"YOU CAN BE GORGEOUS AT THIRTY, CHARMING AT FORTY, AND IRRESISTIBLE FOR THE REST OF YOUR LIFE."

Coco Chanel

THE WILD WOMAN

WEAR RAW TRIMS AND TEXTURED FABRICS TO AWAKEN THE WILD WOMAN WITHIN.

There is a freedom to the Wild Woman – this archetype will reconnect you with the primal rhythms of your soul. She boldly defies conventions that are inauthentic and instead charts her own course. She navigates life with a confidence driven by her deep instinct and unbreakable bond with the living world – informed by the pull of the moon and the whisper of the wind.

*

At Chanel, their use of raw edges, frayed hems and distressed leather speaks to the Wild Woman's embrace of authenticity and rawness. These design elements defy conventional polish, celebrating natural imperfections and the enchantment of the unrefined. This approach mirrors life's inherent messiness and unpredictability, accentuating the beauty found in imperfection.

Coco Chanel was a force of nature, an untamed spirit with a fiercely independent energy. Coco took control of her destiny and forged a path that embraced her femininity while creating her own rules on how that would be achieved. As you connect to the Wild Woman archetype and this untamed aspect of femininity via your clothes, her energy will flow through every thread connecting you to the wild places both inside and around you.

Guidance: Connect to the parts of you that are unwilling to be tamed by letting your hair flow like wild rivers, unrestrained and free. Walk barefoot upon the earth, feeling the planet pulse beneath your feet as you synchronize your body's internal beat to the natural cycles and circadian rhythms of the Earth.

THE MISTRESS

ALLOW RED TO SYMBOLIZE YOUR STRENGTH, CONFIDENCE AND THE UNAPOLOGETIC EXPRESSION OF YOUR DESIRES.

The Mistress archetype embodies themes of femininity, power and allure. Coco Chanel's visionary designs and her unapologetic attitude exemplify this archetype: a woman who commands respect and admiration wherever she goes. Wear red boldly, embodying the essence of a sovereign ruler of your destiny, commanding respect and admiration wherever you tread.

*

Wear your confidence like a cloak, and let your intuition lead you. And of course, complete your look with a Chanel red lip. Coco's love for red lipstick was well-known, and she held strong opinions about make-up and its role in your personal presentation. She believed that make-up was not just about vanity but about enhancing your appearance in a way that exuded confidence and style. Coco herself was seldom seen without carefully applied make-up and her trademark vermilion red lips, which became synonymous with the Chanel brand, and prominently featured in their runway shows and campaigns.

A rich spectrum of Chanel rouge lipstick hues live on, each with its own distinct character. The iconic "Gabrielle" is a vibrant, contemporary red with a subtle golden shimmer. "Pirate", with its classic deep red and blue undertones, exudes timeless Hollywood glamour. In contrast, "La Sensuelle" offers a deep, muted red with sensual, understated elegance.

Affirmation: "I don't chase. I attract."

"WHERE DO YOU WANT TO FLY TO? DRESS FOR THE JOURNEY AND TAKE FLIGHT."

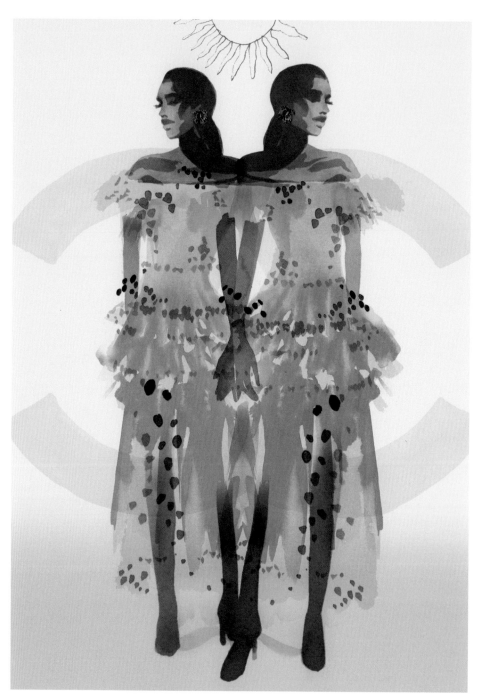

THE LOVER

LET DELICATE FABRICS CARESS YOUR SKIN, ALLOWING ROMANTIC SHEER DETAILS TO HINT AT THE MYSTERY BENEATH.

Embrace feminine silhouettes that accentuate your curves and celebrate your divine form, choosing delicate fabrics that effortlessly flow. Witness a sense of oneness between you and your clothes as you envelop yourself in their soft, silky and delicate textures that not only caress the skin but also symbolize the gentle connection of energies between you and your clothes.

*

Coco Chanel's love life saw each lover play a crucial role in shaping her empire. Arthur "Boy" Capel, her great love, was an English polo player (emphasis on *player*) whom she adored, and he bankrolled her first millinery boutique. Étienne Balsan introduced her to the world of high society, providing her first client base. It was through the Grand Duke Dmitri Pavlovich of Russia that Coco met the perfumer behind the iconic Chanel N°5, while Hugh Grosvenor, the 2nd Duke of Westminster, inspired her love of tweed.

When we let love in, an expansion takes place in the body. Are you aware there is a correlation between the depths we are able to love others and our ability to love ourselves? To what depth are you able to love yourself and let love in? Together, lovers help expand each other, to uplift one another and facilitate a mutual growth of transformation.

Guidance: Do you believe in the power of love? Move through the day sending rays of love to strangers and feel your own heart space soften and expand with every beam of love you send out.

CHANCE

A DROP OF LIFE IN A BOTTLE IS ALL YOU NEED TODAY TO EMBODY THE ENERGY OF SPONTANEOUS CHANCE.

You have connected with the Chance archetype because you are being asked to take a chance on yourself and embrace the serendipitous moments that define a life well-lived. Seize the moment and sail into uncharted territory, for the best opportunities often arise for those willing to take a chance. Make this your lucky day as you open yourself up to adventure, openness and the infinite possibilities that unfold when you surrender to the magic of the universe. That *chance* moment, that *chance* meeting, that *chance* kiss, and that leap taken that changes everything.

*

The Chance scent was created in 2002. It captures the essence of youthful positivity and the thrill of the unexpected, bringing to life a scent that's both playful and sophisticated. The fragrance's name "Chance" perfectly encapsulates the spirit of spontaneity and is designed for the wearer who believes in the power of fate.

As Karl Lagerfeld said: "I don't think a woman is well dressed unless she is wearing perfume." Choose a fragrance that dances playfully on your skin, radiating confidence and flair. Let it announce your arrival before your presence is seen, shifting the mood and altering the frequency of the spaces you enter. Wear your chosen fragrance like a second skin – your personal armour, your signature and a silent declaration of your bold optimism.

Guidance: Dance with uncertainty and find joy in the journey rather than the destination. Let the rhythm of spontaneity and synchronicity lead you to new horizons.

THE COQUETTE

OPT FOR THE PURITY OF WHITE, CHOOSING LIGHT, FLOWING MATERIALS THAT DANCE WITH YOU AS YOU FLIRT WITH LIFE.

The Coquette dances with the energy of intrigue, embracing life's pleasures with a light-hearted spirit and a touch of seduction, flirting with the world that orbits her. You are encouraged to embody the Coquette archetype with a sense of playfulness, charm and confidence, embracing the art of flirtation and allure in a graceful manner as you suggest a hint of innocence to your ensemble to effortlessly capture everyone's attention and leave a lasting impression.

*

When used with precision, the visual impact of white can provide clarity and intention. It's a colour that invites you to embrace simplicity as the ultimate sophistication. Coco Chanel believed white was symbolic of innocence and purity, yet could also be applied to transform an evening dress to hold an aura of seduction. In her hands, white became both a statement of effortless grace and subtle seduction. It is a blank slate and a bold declaration, capturing the Coquette's ability to blend allure with an almost innocent sophistication.

Guidance: Observe the beauty in simplicity and find joy in the small moments – it will bring a sense of peace to your being. You will know you've achieved this by a newfound lightness in your breath and body.

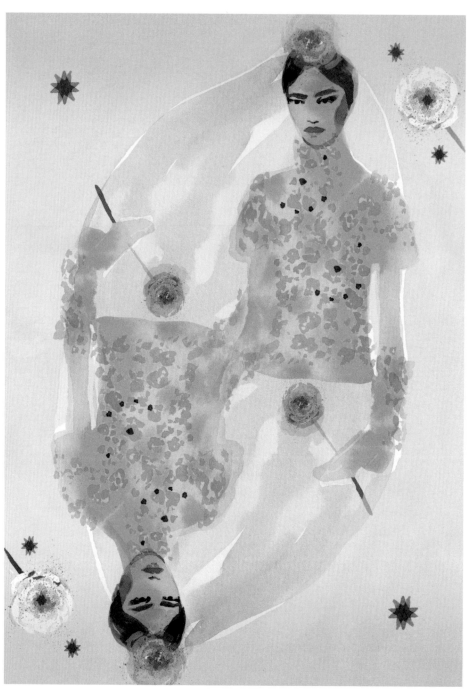

THE MADEMOISELLE

PLAY WITH PROPORTIONS AND CHOOSE ICE CREAM PASTEL HUES OF POWDERY BLUE AND SOFT PINK TO INFUSE A YOUTHFUL TOUCH.

D on't forget the importance of play! When you play, there are no rules – it's your permission slip to be free. Wear clothes that reflect your child-like charm to connect to the Mademoiselle archetype as you bring to life your independent, spirited and rebellious nature.

*

Karl Lagerfeld was known for exaggerating elements of Chanel's classic silhouettes and playing with proportions, creating a dramatic contrast to the garment's more fitted structure. Embrace these dress codes to awaken any dormant desires of freedom within you.

The press often referred to Coco Chanel by the title "Mademoiselle" ("Miss") or "La Grande Mademoiselle" ("The Great"), both intended as terms of respect. This was particularly prominent in her later years, not only to honour her unmarried status but also as a term of endearment used by those close to her.

Guidance: Stop being so serious! The soul finds the lightness of joy through play and you are being urged to return to your true essence through the act of playing. Take cues from children by observing their ease and abandonment of life through their prioritization of play.

THE RAINBOW

DRESS IN THE FULL SPECTRUM OF COLOURS, REFLECTING EVERY FRAGMENT OF LIGHT, AND CELEBRATING ALL FACETS OF YOUR BEING.

Your relationship with wearing colour is an indicator of your relationship with being seen. Does wearing colour make you feel uncomfortable? Strengthen your connection to colour by acknowledging and honouring the diverse aspects of your entire being – recognizing how each aspect of self contributes to the vibrant spectrum of who you are.

*

While the House of Chanel's signature style leans towards a notably restrained colour palette, the brand has experimented with a rainbow spectrum of colours across various collections. These collections feature tweeds and knits with multicoloured threads, soft pastels and sunny hues. Should you choose to dress in a kaleidoscope of colour, you choose to represent every facet of your being, calling back all parts of your identity in this vibrant display. Calling all the fragments of who you are together in one masterpiece outfit gives you access to *all* your power and *all* of your being.

Meditation: Connect to the different facets that you hold with a rainbow meditation. Find a quiet space and meditate on each colour of the rainbow one by one, starting with red and ending with violet. As you immerse yourself in each hue, allow its energy to permeate your being, fostering balance and inner harmony. Take a moment to reflect on any messages, words or visions that arise as you focus on each colour and embrace this journey of self-discovery as you deepen your connection with the spectrum of emotions and qualities within you.

THE MYSTIC

ADORN YOUR ENSEMBLE WITH A MIX OF CRYSTALS TO SUPPORT THE ENERGY OF THE DAY.

Weaving crystals into the fabric of your outfit with details in the buttons, embroidery or accessories holds a special allure and spiritual significance for the Mystic archetype. They are more than a mere embellishment, they serve as conduits of divine energy and protection, connecting you with the deeper spiritual side of your being and the magic that surrounds you.

*

As well as wearing an abundance of jewellery and crystals, Coco Chanel incorporated imitation gems directly into her garments. These faux crystals, meticulously placed on garments and accessories, added a touch of sparkle and sophistication without compromising on aesthetic integrity. This allowed Chanel to democratize luxury, making glamorous embellishments accessible to a wider audience while maintaining the brand's signature style and prestige.

Meditation: Attune yourself to the energy of crystals. Find a quiet space and hold your chosen crystal in your non-dominant hand, feeling its cool weight against your skin. Close your eyes, then allow your breath to lengthen and slow down as you tune into the crystal's unique vibration. Visualize the crystal's facets capturing and reflecting cosmic wisdom and ancient knowledge. With each inhale, imagine the energy of the crystal enveloping you, gradually raising the frequency of your energy field.

THE CAMELLIA

THE PLACEMENT OF A FLOWER EMBELLISHMENT ALLOWS YOUR INNER STRENGTH TO BLOSSOM QUIETLY.

Flowers hold a unique energetic frequency that can help heal and transform our energy. Camellias are connected to divine feminine qualities of softness, receptivity, and inner beauty. Energetically, camellias help harmonize feminine energy, fostering a sense of elegance, while also promoting empowerment and self-expression.

*

For Coco Chanel the camellia flower wasn't merely a decorative element, it was a symbol of purity, elegance and timeless style. A favourite flower of hers, it has become a recurring motif featured prominently in everything from jewellery to haute couture. Their rounded, symmetrically shaped petals embody the balance Coco sought in her designs. Known for blooming even in winter's chill, the camellia also symbolizes resilience and strength. Just as this flower remains in bloom regardless of the season, Chanel's designs have endured through the decades, unfazed by the shifting winds of fashion trends. Unlike more traditional, heavily scented flowers, the camellia is fragrance-free, aligning with Coco's desire for understated elegance – beauty that does not overwhelm but quietly captivates.

Meditation: To connect with the power of flowers, immerse yourself in their presence. Meditate with a single bloom, observing in detail its colours, scent and form. Inviting their energetic frequency to awaken and connect within you.

THE SEDUCTRESS

PAY ATTENTION TO THE FABRIC AND OPT FOR MATERIALS THAT DRAPE THE BODY LIKE A SECOND SKIN.

To embody the seductress is to lean into your powers of allure and sophistication with just enough mystery so as not to give everything away. It is about captivating attention effortlessly, commanding respect and leaving an impression wherever you go. Opt for silk, satin and cashmere as you let the softness of the fabric caress your skin. Accessorize with restraint, yet purposefully. Adorn yourself with delicate jewellery, a strand of pearls, or a pair of diamond earrings that whisper sophistication and enhance your natural allure without overpowering it.

*

True allure lies in the details. Consider the power of a well-placed slit, a strategic glimpse of lace, or the subtle sway given from a high heel. It is in these small, understated gestures that the Seductress archetype truly comes to life. And do not forget the power of confidence. Carry yourself with poise and self-assurance – something Coco Chanel embodied in spades, for it is confidence that truly captivates the hearts and minds of those around you.

Journalling prompt: Write yourself a love letter and list all the ways in which your brilliance shines, affirming your unique qualities that make you truly exceptional. Don't hold back. This isn't showing off – this is showing gratitude for all that you have achieved and all the desirable qualities that you hold.

THE STAR

YOUR TIME TO BE SEEN AND DAZZLE IS NOW – SHINE BRIGHT AND SHOW OFF YOUR STAR QUALITY.

The Star archetype symbolizes inspiration and divine guidance. In tarot the Star card represents hope after hardship, offering optimism and peace by illuminating the darkness and providing clarity and direction.

Wear textures that radiate light as you make your entrance. Shimmer in sequins and reflective materials to strengthen your connection to your inner light. You may hold a fear that your brilliance, when shining bright, could blind those around you. But know that your shine can inspire others to match your vibe and can inspire them to illuminate their light even brighter, for your light paves the way for others (who are also ready to shine) to follow.

*

Coco Chanel had a deep personal connection to the stars. She believed they symbolized luck and destiny, and held a fascination with the constellations and celestial bodies.

Affirmation: "I am ready to remember who I came here to be. I am ready to dial up my light and shine bright."

Tune into your personal North Star to find your direction by visualizing or journalling on the life you wish to create. As you anchor into this vision, ensure that you are the main star in your constellation. Visualize yourself embodying the star qualities you aspire to, and identify the people in your life who make you feel like the star you truly are. Repeat this process daily to embed these star visions into your subconscious. For added magic, visualize while wishing upon a star.

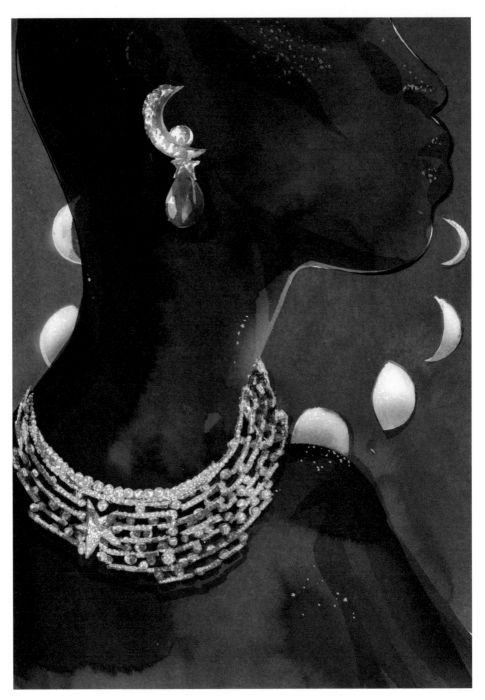

THE MOON

ADD LUNAR SYMBOLISM TO YOUR LOOK AS A POWERFUL SYMBOL OF FEMININITY, INTUITION AND MYSTERY.

Adorn yourself with jewels that capture the energy of the moon – pearls that shimmer like moonlit dew, opals that flicker with lunar iridescence, and silver that echoes the moon's cool embrace. Let your accessories weave the tale of the moon's journey: a crescent moon pendant to herald the growth that follows new beginnings, earrings that cascade like moonlight on water, and bracelets that circle your wrist like lunar orbits.

*

The moon teaches us that change is inevitable. As it waxes and wanes through cycles of new beginnings and endings, so too do our lives flow with similar rhythms. The Chanel brand exemplifies this adaptability, seamlessly embracing new beginnings while preserving its iconic identity. From its inception, Coco Chanel revolutionized fashion by challenging conventions, and this spirit of transformation continued under Karl Lagerfeld, with his vision for reinvention and blending heritage with contemporary flair. His immediate successor, Virginie Viard, was a true guardian of the brand, bringing a romantic sensibility, honouring its storied past and navigating the brand towards the future.

Guidance: Just as the moon reveals its greatest magic in the darkest of nights, so too can you discover your deepest wisdom during your darkest moments. Embrace the phases of the moon as a mirror to support your life's journey; set intentions under the new moon, nurture growth as she waxes, acknowledge and celebrate your achievements on a full moon, and release what no longer serves you as she wanes.

4

THE
ORIGINAL
INFLUENCER

Fashion is a force that can shape reality, not just appearances. When you wear the clothes suggested in this chapter, you are invited not simply to wear them but to embody them as you set a standard that will inspire and influence everyone who crosses your path.

"I DON'T DO FASHION. I AM FASHION."

Coco Chanel

THE IT GIRL

ADOPT A FRENCH IT GIRL UNIFORM TO EFFORTLESSLY EXUDE THAT COOL-GIRL CHIC AND MAKE THIS ENERGY YOUR OWN.

French It Girl chic is the art of effortless elegance, embodying a refined rebel quality that feels both timeless and refreshingly modern and masters the balance between simplicity and sophistication. An approach to style that is utterly personal and entirely natural, capturing the elusive *je ne sais quoi* that the world has long admired. What sets this archetype apart is her attitude – never trying too hard. Her hair is tousled, and her make-up understated, enhancing natural beauty with just a hint of red lipstick and a swipe of mascara.

*

A significant portion of this archetype's wardrobe owes its allure to Coco Chanel. She popularized many of this archetype's wardrobe staples, including the little black dress, the perfectly tailored blazer, the well-crafted crossbody handbag, the iconic ballet pumps, the Breton stripped top, and encouraged you to adopt a colour palette of navy, white, nude, and black with a hint of red on your lips and nails developing the definitive formula for dressing in the energy of this sartorial icon. Always ahead of her time, Coco introduced the striped *marinière* to women's fashion in the 1910s after being inspired by the uniforms of French sailors. Pairing the Breton stripe with her signature elegance and rebellious spirit, she transformed it into a timeless symbol of effortless chic.

Guidance: Bof... just be cool and try less hard.

THE INFLUENCER

BE BOLD, STAND OUT AND OPT FOR A STYLE CHOICE THAT IS SURE TO INFLUENCE OTHERS TO FOLLOW.

The Influencer knows that their style is a visual narrative. From bold statement pieces to everyday basics, each item is chosen with intent to reflect their personal brand.

*

The Influencer seeks pieces that not only spotlight their unique style but will also turn heads. The audacious Hula Hoop Bag, from Spring/Summer 2013 – an oversized, avant-garde accessory, is not for the faint of heart. With its dramatic proportions and playful design, this bag is a bold statement piece that commands attention and showcases a fearless approach to fashion. These bold, one-of-a-kind Chanel pieces are made for those who aren't following trends – they're setting them.

Coco Chanel was the original influencer, reshaping fashion and society with her revolutionary ideas. While the term influencer may not have existed during her time, her impact is undeniable and her influence extends far beyond mere trends.

Prioritize a distinct signature style to curate your look and reflect this authentically. Develop signature pieces or looks that become synonymous with your style. Whether it's bold make-up, a statement coat or a penchant for monochrome dressing, having a style signature makes you instantly recognizable. Always be camera-ready and dress with the lens in mind. Understand the power of a good photo and consider how your outfit will translate on camera.

Guidance: Clinging to the familiar and the tested will only anchor you in the shadows of what has already been. To transcend and advance, you must move towards the uncharted and the new.

THE TASTEMAKER

ADORN YOUR HAIR WITH A CHIC VELVET BOW OR ADD DRAMA TO YOUR SILHOUETTE AND GO OVERSIZED.

Much like the final flourish on a present, there is intentionality when you add a bow to your outfit – a deliberate accent that adds personality and flair. Whether it's a delicate, petite bow on a blouse or an oversized and dramatic addition to your form, it signals the wearer clearly understands the power of a simple yet powerful detail that transforms an entire look.

*

Just like Coco Chanel before you, connecting to the Tastemaker archetype means you have a keen understanding of fashion and a willingness to curate unique, compelling looks. Coco took a simple bow and elevated its status from a nostalgic nod to heritage, to super chic as she gave it an updated modern sensibility. The bow has become a hallmark of Chanel and a signature detail.

There is duality in the energy of a bow – it's a symbol of innocent playfulness, yet its placement offers the utmost elegance as it strikes a balance of soft and eye-catching. A bow evokes femininity but also carries a certain boldness, drawing attention to its wearer with a touch of whimsy, and a promise of a gift to be unwrapped.

Guidance: Romanticize the mundane by seeing the sacred in the ordinary. Transform routine into the divine; your shower becomes a private concert hall, a cup of coffee turns into an artisan creation, cleaning becomes an act of love for your home, and your daily commute becomes a mini escape.

THE TRENDSETTER

BLEND REAL GEMS ALONGSIDE COSTUME JEWELLERY TO BALANCE THE MATERIAL AND THE ETHEREAL.

Coco Chanel's keen sense of what women wanted in their wardrobes was led by her own impeccable taste. Seldom seen without her signature jewellery, Coco liked the way a string of pearls could emphasize a sun-kissed glow against the skin, while she also believed they held the ability to highlight a sparkle in the eyes.

There was no sense of hierarchy when it came to the bijoux in her jewellery box. In fact, Coco often favoured costume pieces over real gems, finding the real thing to be ostentatious. Gifted many extravagant jewels from boyfriends and lovers, Coco often paired these alongside glimmering glass beads. She made jewellery part of her daily life, wearing pieces just as naturally while hunting in the countryside as she did lounging on the beach.

Coco's costume jewellery is not just an accessory; it's an attitude. A statement that adorns both body and soul. It's the perfect blend of accessible glamour and timeless sophistication and proof that true style transcends the value of materials.

Coco embodies the Trendsetter archetype, setting the fashion pace that the world continues to follow. Her work is a testament to the transformative power of style, setting trends and shaping cultural conversations.

Guidance: We don't just hear things to be true, they are felt deeply. When something resonates on a soul level, the goosebumps you experience are these truths vibrating through you. Tune into the frequency of these sensations to recognize which conversations connect to your soul's essence.

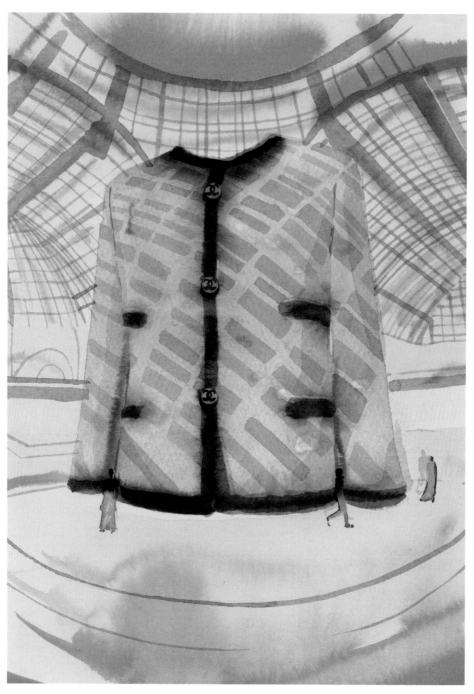

THE ICON

DRESS WITH DELIBERATE FLAIR AND OPT FOR TAILORED PIECES WITH CLEAN LINES AND ELEGANT SILHOUETTES.

The magnetic energy of the Icon archetype effortlessly draws people in with its charisma. Dress in elements found in the iconic Chanel suit to connect to this archetype. Introduced in the early 1920s this revolutionary design set a new standard for elegance and comfort. Characterized by its collarless jacket and fitted skirt, often crafted from luxurious tweed, this suit was celebrated for its timeless style and the ease of movement it offered the wearer. Meticulous attention to detail is evident in the gold chain sewn into the inner seams, ensuring the fabric drapes perfectly and guarantees a precise silhouette.

*

For over a century, this Chanel suit has served as the uniform for countless Icons, embodying instant elegance and practicality. Its crease-resistant tweed made it ideal for the jet set on their long-haul flights, ensuring the wearer arrived impeccably fresh-looking. From Princess Diana and Jackie Kennedy to Grace Kelly, Marilyn Monroe, and Brigitte Bardot, these influential women were devoted fans of Chanel, both on and off-screen. This further contributed to the brand's status as a symbol of luxury, sophistication and iconic style.

Karl Lagerfeld's runway show for Spring/Summer 2008 featured models walking in and around a giant, oversized three-dimensional Chanel jacket. This was a dramatic and symbolic tribute to Coco, serving as a larger-than-life representation of the house's iconic jacket.

Affirmation: *"Everything that I do makes an impact. My every action, thought and breath is important."*

"BE THE
ARCHITECT OF
YOUR ENERGY
BY BUILDING
YOUR
FREQUENCY
VIA YOUR
OUTFIT."

THE CREATOR

REACH FOR TWEED THAT FEATURES RICH TEXTURES AND SUBTLE COLOUR VARIATIONS.

Tuning into your passions gives you access to the Creator archetype. Learn to create in all conditions. To create consistently, you must reinvest your creative energies despite the setbacks that life may present. Recognize what makes you feel alive, as this will enhance your life force.

*

At Chanel, tweed transcends mere fabric to become a defining element of the brand's legacy, embodying Coco Chanel's vision of effortless elegance. Coco introduced tweed into her collections in the early 1920s. This material was a bold departure from the restrictive textiles of the time – she chose it for its unparalleled comfort and chic simplicity. Coco's pioneering use of tweed, often seen in her iconic suits, revolutionized women's fashion by combining traditional masculine textiles with feminine silhouettes. The fabric's resilience and sophisticated texture not only ensured that garments draped perfectly but also maintained their allure over time. With its rich heritage and timeless appeal, tweed remains synonymous with Chanel's ethos of understated luxury and impeccable craftsmanship.

Karl Lagerfeld modernized traditional tweed once more by infusing it with vibrant colours, metallic threads and unconventional materials, creating a fantasy-like reinvention of the classic fabric.

Affirmation: "I have the ability to create and I choose to create the life I desire."

THE ARTIST

PAINT YOUR SARTORIAL CANVAS WITH CREATIVE EXPRESSION, COLOUR AND TEXTURE WITH LASER PRECISION.

The Artist archetype channels divine inspiration into earthly creations. A process of dancing on the edge of the metaphysical, translating messages from the cosmos into a tangible art form, earthside. Through their creations the artist can awaken dormant beauty within the observer. Art can provoke, inspire and delight as the eye takes in these crafted forms. Memories can resurface, fresh ideas can ignite and dormant emotions awaken.

*

Coco Chanel is renowned for her attention to detail. Experiment with fringe features for added movement, incorporate cut-out details to paint a modern twist to a classic silhouette, or add contrast piping for a subtle effect that highlights the garment's silhouette.

Coco's circle of artist friends was a dazzling constellation of creativity and style. From the visionary poet and filmmaker Jean Cocteau to the pioneering artist Salvador Dalí, Coco surrounded herself with luminaries. Her work with these figures infused her designs with a unique blend of artistic flair and innovation. Their influence created a synergy that propelled Coco's fashion to new heights, blending the realms of high art and haute couture.

Affirmation: "I am enough."

Release the chains of perfectionism. If you find yourself crippled by its grip, know that it stems from a time when revealing your true self felt perilous. Embrace imperfection as a gateway to authenticity and create with a freedom unburdened by fear.

THE LEGEND

CHOOSE TIMELESS ACCESSORIES THAT RESONATE DEEPLY WITH YOUR SPIRIT AND WILL BE CHERISHED THROUGH THE GENERATIONS.

The Legend archetype embodies the essence of lasting influence and iconic status, representing individuals whose impact transcends time and cultural shifts. Legends are celebrated not just for their achievements but for their ability to inspire and redefine the standards of their era. They leave a lasting legacy through their distinctive vision and groundbreaking contributions.

*

Coco Chanel has a place in fashion history as one of the immortals, not merely as a designer but as a transformative force whose ideas continue to resonate. From her revolutionary designs, like the iconic little black dress and the timeless Chanel suit, to her visionary reinvention of humble tweed and a bold reimagining of women's fashion, Coco set new standards that redefined elegance. She understood the impact that fashion has, and her influence reshaped the very essence of feminine style and empowerment.

Coco's enduring legacy continues to shape the fashion industry and influence contemporary designers, influencers and tastemakers. The Chanel brand remains one of the most recognizable and revered names in fashion, synonymous with timeless elegance, innovation and sophistication.

> *Guidance: Prepare for your legacy by regularly reflecting on the impact you wish to have on this world and how you can align your daily actions with that vision. Consider how you want to be remembered and take steps towards that reality.*

THE PROPHET

CARRY THE IMPRINT OF YOUR NUMEROLOGICAL PATH OR YOUR LUCKY NUMBER TO CONNECT TO HIGHER TRUTHS.

The Prophet is a catalyst for social change and transformation, advocating for equality and human rights. Make a lasting impact as you share your message and mission today and weave in symbols of enlightenment and transformation. In the knowledge that a higher power guides and protects you, have the courage to share your beliefs even in the face of opposition or adversity.

*

Coco Chanel was reportedly open to mystical guidance and believed in the power of numbers, particularly her lucky number five, which corresponded to her zodiac house in astrology (she was a Leo). Coco's collections often debuted on the fifth day of the month – and, of course, it is the number which adorns the bottle of her first fragrance, Chanel N°5. In numerology, the number 5 is associated with change, freedom and adventure. It represents versatility, courage and the ability to adapt to various situations. This aligns with Coco's pioneering spirit in fashion and her desire to liberate women from restrictive clothing norms as she redefined what it meant to be a modern woman in that era.

Guidance: Connect to the wisdom of numerology by discovering the meaning of your Life Path Number.

Your Life Path Number serves as a blueprint for understanding your journey and making informed decisions aligned with your purpose and direction. See overleaf to calculate your own.

Life Path Numbers are based on ancient wisdom guiding people to find new meaning, purpose and direction. This method is part of the broader system of numerology which traces back to ancient civilizations including the Babylonians, Greek philosophers and mathematicians, and early Egyptians. It's a system that links numbers to cosmic principles, spiritual meaning and personal characteristics.

To discover your Life Path Number, start by adding together the digits of your birth day, month and year separately (D + D + M + M + Y + Y + Y + Y). Continue adding these digits together until you reach a single digit between 1 and 9, or one of the master numbers 11, 22 or 33. For example, by adding together the numbers of Karl Lagerfeld's birth date (10/09/1933), we get $1 + 0 + 0 + 9 + 1 + 9 + 3 + 3 = 26$, and further adding $2 + 6 = 8$, revealing Karl's Life Path Number is 8.

✦ **LIFE PATH 1: THE LEADER** – Bold and unstoppable, a natural leader driven to break new ground and claim the spotlight. Although you may feel isolated at times, use that space for self-reflection.

✦ **LIFE PATH 2: THE DIPLOMAT** – The elegant peacemaker. Your superpower is bringing people together and creating harmony. Just remember to prioritize your own needs too.

✦ **LIFE PATH 3: THE CREATIVE** – Charming and romantic, you're life's unofficial hype person. Full of creative energy, it flows through your veins! Balance this with spiritual depth to uncover meaningful life experiences.

✦ **LIFE PATH 4: THE BUILDER** – Dedicated and down to earth, you lay the foundations of stability with an unmatched work ethic. Embrace flexibility and change to unlock your full potential.

✦ **LIFE PATH 5: THE ADVENTURER** – Free-spirited, your heart is always tugging towards the next adventure. Life is never boring around you – you're sociable by nature, but it can be hard to let others get close.

✦ **LIFE PATH 6: THE NURTURER** – Your heart is your compass, guiding you to uplift everyone with your warm energy. You create loving spaces where others thrive and feel truly seen. Balance giving and receiving.

✦ **LIFE PATH 7: THE SEEKER** – Both book-smart and mystically wise. Forever diving deep into life's mysteries and finding wisdom in the quiet corners of the world. Trust your inner guidance.

✦ **LIFE PATH 8: THE ACHIEVER** – The boss. Powerful and ambitious, you're destined for success, influence and abundance. Find the harmony between ambition and compassion.

✦ **LIFE PATH 9: THE HUMANITARIAN** – A social justice warrior with a heart bigger than your to-do list, saving the world one gesture at a time. Learn that asking for help isn't a burden.

✦ **LIFE PATH 11: THE VISIONARY** – Intuitive and often psychic. You have a beautiful soul that attracts others to you. Both confident and prone to worry, learn to trust and harness your gifts.

✦ **LIFE PATH 22: THE ARCHITECT** – Your work ethic to support humankind is unmatched. Part visionary, part CEO, you're the person who turns wild ideas into actual things – like, you know, pyramids or global startups. Stay grounded.

✦ **LIFE PATH 33: TEACHER OF TEACHERS** – You radiate love and wisdom. This rare Life Path may take a lifetime to master, with challenges designed to awaken your gifts as a spiritual leader and healer. Boundaries are essential.

THE WISDOM KEEPER

ACCESSORIZE WITH YOUR WORD, WISDOM AND INTUITION WHILE SAFEGUARDING THE POWER OF YOUR THROAT CHAKRA TODAY.

Wear a scarf or necklace to shield your throat chakra, an important energy centre within the energy body. Take extra care when delivering your words today as you speak your truth with confidence – speaking into reality your deepest desires, creative visions, or setting personal boundaries. When your throat chakra is flowing with ease, you will speak these words while exuding a magnetic and grounded sense of presence. A balanced throat chakra ensures that your words are a genuine reflection of your soul's intent and that you are not simply echoing what the world around you expects to hear.

*

Coco Chanel was audacious, bold and brave as she imparted knowledge that no one else dared and shared this wisdom to create new realms leading to the world of fashion we live in today.

Guidance: Do not swallow your words for fear of being misunderstood. This can create tension and a build-up of energy as all the words left unsaid get stuck in your throat chakra. It may not be easy, but it is safe to speak your truth. Much like strengthening any muscle, the more you practise, the easier this will become. If it is not possible to speak these words directly, consider communicating them and letting this energy leave the body via the act of writing a letter. The intention is not necessarily to send the letter. You can rip it up, burn or bury it. Speak from the heart with love and compassion for both yourself and those receiving your words.

THE PIERROT

UNLEASH THE POTENTIAL OF THE COLLAR, FOR IT HOLDS THE KEY TO YOUR EXPRESSION.

The Pierrot archetype, often associated with the Fool card in traditional tarot decks, represents new beginnings, innocence and spontaneity. Evoke this energy by exploring ruffle details, pleats and frilled collars to further enhance a playful and whimsical aesthetic. Whether you choose classic simplicity or bold embellishment, let it define your neckline and frame your face, enhancing your entire silhouette.

*

Both Karl Lagerfeld and Coco Chanel elevated the importance of a collar in an outfit.

Coco simplified and modernized traditional collar styles as she favoured clean lines and understated elegance. The classic Chanel tweed jacket featured a notched collar – a small cut-out or "notch" where the collar meets the lapel, creating a distinct V-shaped indentation which adds a clean, geometric structure. Coco was also known for collarless designs, particularly in her iconic jersey suits and dresses. These were a radical departure from traditional fashion norms as she emphasized a clean, streamlined look.

By contrast, Lagerfeld added drama to the Chanel collar. He often experimented with oversized collars, asymmetrical shapes and unique fabric combinations. He frequently embellished collars with intricate details such as beading, embroidery and appliqué. These embellishments added a touch of luxury and craftsmanship to the garments, elevating the overall aesthetic.

Guidance: Allow yourself to enjoy new beginnings with an open heart, unburdened from the weight of past experiences or fears, and fully enjoy this new journey ahead filled with endless possibilities.

THE LEADING LADY

LET YOUR STYLE COMMAND ATTENTION AND LET YOUR AURA RADIATE CONFIDENCE.

D ress to be seen with the energy of the Hollywood Leading Ladies that Coco Chanel designed for. Opt for impeccably tailored pieces that ensure a flawless fit and elevate your look with a touch of dramatic flair: a bold lip, or a flowing scarf – these elements should enhance, not overshadow your inherent elegance.

*

The epitome of grace and poise, Grace Kelly regularly wore Chanel and was a testament to the house's refined elegance. Her style exuded the quiet luxury that Chanel perfected. Elizabeth Taylor, known for her opulent jewellery and dramatic roles, often gravitated towards the chic simplicity of Chanel in her off-screen style. Meanwhile, Marlene Dietrich, a symbol of femme fatale allure, was a devoted fan of Chanel's androgynous, streamlined silhouettes. Marilyn Monroe's association with the brand transcended clothing; her famous declaration that she wore nothing but Chanel Nº5 to bed immortalized both the actress and the fragrance in popular culture.

Coco's relationships with celebrities and socialites helped to create her brand's association with luxury and high society.

But it was Coco's influence on Hollywood's most iconic leading ladies that cemented her place as a fashion legend.

Affirmation: "It is safe to be seen in the entirety of my being. I bring into focus any parts of myself that I have been hiding and send it my unconditional love, allowing these aspects to understand on a cellular level that there is no need to hide." Release any fears holding you back from being seen.

THE COSMIC VOYAGER

BLEND LUXURIOUS MATERIALS WITH AN ATHLETIC AESTHETIC TO ACHIEVE AN ELEGANT CELESTIAL LOOK.

W/hen travelling through space and time, past planets, constellations and shooting stars, harmonize opulent fabrics with a sporty edge to combine both elegance and energy into your attire.

*

Karl Lagerfeld first made the blend of a luxury sporty aesthetic famous in his City Surfer runway show for Spring/Summer 1991. Those who witnessed this iconic moment saw legendary supermodel Linda Evangelista walk down the runway carrying a CC branded surfboard and a wetsuit-shaped sequin jacket that had a sporty zip-up fastening. Both Coco Chanel and Lagerfeld designed for the modern woman of their era, and Lagerfeld recognized that the women he was designing for in the 90s were now sexier and sportier. He designed a collection to cater to this, pairing tweed jackets with trainers and tracksuits made from luxury materials. Fusing high fashion and sportswear became part of Chanel's modern design ethos.

Meditation: Are you unclear on your journey ahead? Choose your mode of transport and visualize yourself travelling through space and time. Connect into Stellar Consciousness by deeply connecting to the cosmic and celestial aspects that you see around you as you sink into a higher sense of awareness. This meditative journey can reveal to you where you desire to go, professionally or personally. Ask the galactic universe that surrounds you to bring to mind the places that you need to go and the people that will support you on that journey.

THE CELESTIAL BEING

YOUR AURA EMANATES A RADIANT LIGHT THAT ILLUMINATES YOUR SURROUNDINGS.

O pt for materials that enhance your aura's light with metallic finishes. Incorporate shimmering silvers and ethereal whites that evoke the celestial realm, or fabrics that sparkle like starlight and capture the iridescence of our galaxies. As you adopt this archetype, the invitation is to wear garments that convey a sense of weightlessness, mirroring your connection to the infinite expanse of space. You may connect to the Celestial Being archetype for your profound wisdom and cosmic insights feel otherworldly, and you find yourself serving as a guide or messenger, imparting these divine truths to humanity.

*

Equally, Coco Chanel's ideas may have seemed out of this world, transcending earthly norms as she landed visionary concepts that transformed the fashion universe. Her ideas on redefining femininity through fashion continue to play a part on our planet, influencing how we dress more than a century later.

To activate your galactic remembrance, use this affirmation:
"I am a child of the stars. My cosmic being holds memories ready to be awakened as my heart returns home to the galaxy."

Connect with the rhythms of the cosmos by taking part in traditions that honour celestial events, such as lunar phases or planetary alignments.

5

POWER DRESSING

In order to make a powerful impact on this planet, you must be comfortable with the power that you hold. Engage with this power by adopting the dress codes shared by the archetypes in this chapter, for the colours, symbolism and silhouettes they suggest are not merely fashion statements – they are tools for transformation.

"SWEATPANTS ARE A SIGN OF DEFEAT. YOU LOST CONTROL OF YOUR LIFE, SO YOU BOUGHT SOME SWEATPANTS."

Karl Lagerfeld

THE GODDESS

LET YOUR JEWELLERY SPEAK THE LANGUAGE OF THE EGYPTIAN GODS.

Attune to the essence of the Goddess' divine power by embellishing yourself with Egyptian symbols of protection and divine favour – amulets of ankhs, scarabs and the Eye of Horus to access a connection to all aspects of your wisdom, beauty and a deep knowing of your place in the world. This archetype celebrates the power of the feminine in all its forms – creation, destruction, protection, nurturing and wisdom. Honour the feminine aspects within you, however you identify, and understand that true strength often comes from qualities like empathy, intuition and the ability to nurture life.

*

Karl Lagerfeld's Métiers d'Art 2018/2019 collection, presented at the Metropolitan Museum of Art in New York, is perhaps the most striking homage to the Goddess archetype with a direct nod to ancient Egypt. The collection brought the timeless allure of Egyptian goddesses to the modern runway. Gold – a symbol of immortality and divine beauty – dominated the collection, shimmering across dresses, skirts and accessories with an opulence that evoked the sun god Ra himself. Lagerfeld channelled the Goddess archetype, drawing inspiration from Isis, Hathor and other deities of ancient myth. Structured garments reminiscent of the robes of pharaohs featured intricate beadwork and hieroglyphic motifs, while flowing capes and high collars added drama. Each piece told a story of power, beauty and eternal femininity, elevating the wearer to a status that was nothing short of divine.

Guidance: Surround yourself with people who recognize your worth. Equally important is recognizing your own value.

THE MAIDEN

ANCHOR YOURSELF IN DURABLE DENIM AS YOU PREPARE FOR EVERY EVOLVING ADVENTURE THAT COMES YOUR WAY.

The Maiden archetype represents youthful vitality, fresh beginnings and a vibrant spirit. She embodies the qualities of innocence, curiosity and potential. When it comes to style, the Maiden's choice of denim is both symbolic and practical, aligning perfectly with her adventurous spirit and her readiness to embrace the world with an open heart. Denim's enduring quality and ability to adapt from day to night speaks to the Maiden's inclination towards both practicality and style, allowing her to seamlessly transition through the various stages of her journey.

*

At Chanel, denim is more than just a fabric; it captures the brand's signature blend of sophistication and rebellion. By reinterpreting this classic fabric with a chic, modern sensibility Chanel transforms denim from a staple of casual wear into a symbol of fresh, daring style. Whether a tailored jacket or a full denim-on-denim look, Chanel's designs reflect the Maiden's spirited grace.

The Maiden represents a stage in personal development that is open to growth and transformation. In essence, she is about embracing life with enthusiasm, seeking new experiences and staying true to your inner potential. She symbolizes the beauty of youth and the excitement of embarking on a new journey with a heart full of hope and a spirit eager to explore.

Guidance: Adopt a beginner's mindset to learning and approach challenges without the burden of preconceived expectations. Anything is possible as a beginner, unlock your endless potential.

THE LIONESS

CHOOSE SHADES OF GOLD AND CREAM, AND DRESS WITH COURAGE AND AUDACITY.

Wrap yourself in regal golden tones, and face the world with the fierce bravery and majestic heart of the Lioness. Discover the spiritual guidance of the Lioness archetype that inspired Coco Chanel on her path, and it can inspire you in yours.

There is a strength and boldness in this archetype, a potent symbol of feminine power. Connect with this energy to help establish necessary boundaries, for the Lioness intuitively knows when to assert herself; when to snarl and show her teeth to defend her space, and when to roar with her full power. She challenges stereotypes of passive femininity, instead embodying assertiveness, resilience and a fierce spirit. The Lioness archetype inspires women to embrace their inner strength, assert their boundaries and pursue their goals with determination. They symbolize the instinctual drive to safeguard loved ones and defend what is important. In the human psyche, the Lioness archetype represents nurturing and protective instincts, advocating for those in their care with unwavering dedication.

Within a pride, lionesses often take on leadership roles in hunting and caring for the group. They exhibit both an independence and a cooperative spirit, working together for the collective good.

Reflection: When the world has you snarling and growling, ask yourself: "Does it matter?" Tap into your inner strength and use your energy strategically, saving it to protect what matters most.

Reflect on what's louder?
The roars of society – or the whispers of your heart?

THE EMPRESS

TAP INTO THE FEMININE ASPECTS OF YOUR ENERGY.

Opt for feminine frills and florals, but don't forget to complete your look with jewellery to signify your status as a divine being. In the tarot, the Empress is depicted wearing symbols of nature – leaves, flowers and vines – that represent fertility and the cycles of life. She is surrounded by wheat (a favourite symbol of Coco Chanel, representing harvest and abundance) and crowned with stars that signify her connection to the divine. Traditionally depicted as heavily pregnant, the Empress in tarot reflects the potential of new ideas that she will birth into life.

*

The Empress embodies abundance, much as the Chanel brand epitomizes luxury. While Coco's idea of luxury extended past opulence, her ability to blend practicality with luxury reflects the Empress's ability to provide comfort and beauty in a balanced, harmonious way. This archetype mirrors the creative force that Coco channelled throughout her career, celebrating femininity not through the lens of fragility but through strength, independence and sophistication. Coco's designs became emblems of empowered femininity, merging femininity with authority.

Affirmation: "I am ready to receive and enjoy the fruits of my labour. I recognize the abundance that already exists in my life as I step into this chapter of plenty."

Your time to create is right now. You hold all the tools necessary to transform your visions into reality, as prosperity surrounds you, ready for harvest.

171

THE MOTHER

EMBRACE CLOTHES AND ACCESSORIES THAT SHIMMER WITH GOLDEN THREADS.

You have landed on the Mother archetype because your soul may desire tender care, and a loving connection. You may be bringing new life into the world with a new project, service, product or idea – and need to give it some motherly protective support. The divine Mother archetype represents the nurturing, caring and protective aspects of the feminine. At her essence is a deep connection to creation, an energy that is chaotic – able to both birth new life and destroy in the same breath and yet encompasses qualities of compassion, empathy and unconditional love.

*

Dress in clothes that echo the theme of abundance symbolized by wheat; golden threads woven into the texture of the fabric giving a subtle shimmer, golden chains that accentuate your bag or belt, adding a touch of opulence, or incorporate jewellery inspired by the abundant symbol of wheat.

In tarot, wheat signifies abundance with its connotations of harvest and prosperity, which mirrors the mother's role in providing sustenance and growth. Wheat symbols found in Coco's designs weren't just an ornamental choice, they represented the idea of harvest and the promise of growth. Coco, known for her interest in tarot, often used this golden grain in her designs as a metaphor for prosperity.

Reflection: If you hold an instinctive drive to care for others, consider whether you extend the same level of care towards yourself. Are you nurturing your own needs and desires with the same dedication and enthusiasm you offer others?

THE ELDER

LET YOUR FEET GUIDE YOU – CHOOSE YOUR SHOES FIRST, FOR THEY ARE THE FOUNDATION OF YOUR JOURNEY AHEAD.

Dress from the feet up. The Elder archetype reflects a life lived, guiding others with accumulated wisdom and style. Having walked further on the path, the Elder understands the importance of choosing footwear that will take you to where you want to go. The energy of your shoes will set the tone for all that follows, grounding your intentions as you walk your path.

*

The iconic two-tone Chanel shoe offers a perfect harmony of form and function. Introduced by Coco Chanel in the 1950s, it remains a pinnacle of sophisticated design and timeless elegance. With its sleek, streamlined silhouette and contrasting hues – typically a black toe paired with a neutral or beige heel – the shoe epitomizes Coco's genius for merging practicality with style. The contrast between the neutral body and the darker toe creates an optical illusion, making the leg appear longer and more streamlined. It's a subtle yet powerful detail that transforms the silhouette. This clever classic design also seamlessly blends with any wardrobe, making it a versatile staple.

Follow in the footsteps of Coco and hold your authority with quiet confidence in shoes that embody both elegance and practicality in equal balance.

Reflection: Take time to reflect on the experiences that have shaped you and brought you to this phase of your life journey. Understanding how your past has influenced who you are today can provide clarity on the steps ahead and allow you to celebrate how far you've come.

THE PUNK PRINCESS

EXPLORE THE RELATIONSHIP BETWEEN HARD AND SOFT EDGES TO CHANNEL THE DANCE OF OPPOSING FORCES.

How can you become a Queen if you haven't had your Princess era? Embrace the enchantment of fairy tales and create a look that is both grounded and ethereal. The Punk Princess will reject conventional standards of beauty and be bold, unconventional and unapologetically unique – to add an edge to whimsy, add a touch of your inner rebel. The Princess archetype represents new beginnings and hope; her journey is one of transformation from innocence to wisdom. To embody this potential for growth, dress with the balance of power and serenity, for this contrast mirrors the duality within and around you, inviting an energy that holds both resilience and ease.

*

During Karl Lagerfeld's tenure as creative director at Chanel, he famously created a captivating juxtaposition of rebellion and refinement in the early 1990s. The interplay of textures is central to this theme. Think distressed leather jackets adorned with intricate beadwork or spikes juxtaposed with softer, more luxurious materials such as tulle skirts. Contrasting punk influences such as studs, chains and pins and reimagining them through the Chanel lens, Lagerfeld integrated these accents into elegant silhouettes, bridging the gap between punk's raw edge and high fashion's refined aesthetic, creating a final look that was equally fierce and feminine.

Affirmation for prosperity: "I am a magnet for abundance and release any blocks – self-imposed or external – that hold me back from receiving." Receiving is your birthright.

THE DEVIL

EVERY FASHION CHOICE TODAY MUST BE DELIBERATE; FOR, AS YOU KNOW, THE *DEVIL* IS IN THE *DETAIL*.

L et go of the unhealthy addiction to fleeting trends and seize control of your look. Resist the temptation to depend on the latest fads, and let every thread you wear speak with purpose – for it is in the subtle, unseen details that your true power and presence will be known. The Devil archetype embodies dominance, confidence and control, carrying an air of authority. As you dress in the energy of this archetype, focus on pleasure. You are a temptress – be seductive not just with your appearance but with your words and energy. Opt for pieces where the details do the talking. It's the thoughtful nuances that make your look memorable and elevate even the simplest outfit into something utterly captivating.

*

Coco Chanel's refusal to lean on passing trends underscores her belief in the power of personal style and the importance of investing in pieces that stand the test of time. A piece from Chanel consistently offers a classic timeless authority with a strong presence that isn't seduced by a trend.

> *Guidance: Eliminate the word "should" from your vocabulary today. Your actions are driven by desire, not obligation: let that guide you.*

THE DANDY

ELEVATE YOUR NECKWEAR GAME – WHETHER IT'S A BOW, A CRAVAT OR A TIE – TO ADD A LITTLE POLISH, BE IT FOR FASHION OR FUNCTION.

From 1983 until his passing in 2019, Karl Lagerfeld was the creative force behind Chanel. Part of Lagerfeld's genius was his ability to blend the tradition of the Dandy archetype with the ever-evolving world of high fashion.

Lagerfeld was famous for his daily uniform – a study in sartorial precision, which became as iconic as the collections he fashioned. Like Coco before him, he understood the power of a uniform, with his impeccably tailored black suits, crisp white shirts and his ever-present and perfectly coiffed ponytail creating a silhouette that was as sharp as it was unmistakable. Just as Coco had her pearls, Lagerfeld was rarely seen without his signature dark shades, fingerless biker gloves and a stern, enigmatic expression that suggested he was perpetually dissecting the world through a lens of elegance and critique.

Lagerfeld's aesthetic, however, was more than just a uniform; it was a meticulously crafted persona that echoed the spirit of the Dandy archetype. Like the dandies of the late eighteenth and early nineteenth centuries – those arbiters of style and taste who championed elegance as an art form – Lagerfeld understood the power of appearances. His commitment to a consistent, polished image was a modern homage to the Dandy's philosophy: that fashion is not just about clothing but about character. Ultimately, this became part of his legacy.

Guidance: Be precise with your words. Ensure clarity and leave no room for assumptions or misunderstandings.

THE MAGICIAN

GRAVITATE TOWARDS BOLD, EYE-CATCHING PIECES THAT COMMAND ATTENTION AND SPARK INTRIGUE.

The ability to create magic lies in creating something out of nothing – mastering the frequencies of the universe to construct, form, and shape new realities. Be bold with the magic you create and choose an ornate headpiece or elaborate piece of jewellery to finish your look with mystical flair.

*

Karl Lagerfeld's visionary direction of the Chanel runway shows made them legendary. Transforming the Grand Palais in Paris into fantastical settings – from a supermarket to airport terminals – Lagerfeld turned each show into an immersive and theatrical spectacle, transforming even the simplest of themes into magical experiences.

The Magician wields the power to transform the hidden energies within and around you. With the mastery of unseen forces, this archetype creates shifts in your reality, inviting you to harness your potential and shape the world anew. Embrace this power and watch as the ordinary becomes extraordinary.

The Magician archetype can inspire you to bring significant changes to your life instantly. They have everything needed to create; all you need is belief in the outcome and the power of your mind to manifest it.

Affirmation: "I believe in the magic of miracles and their power to transform my life."

THE QUEEN

SHOWER YOURSELF IN AN ABUNDANCE OF JEWELS, GEMS AND CRYSTALS.

Adorn yourself with jewels worthy of a crown. Wear them intentionally, knowing of their value, power and the energy they offer. Focus on the energy of the jewels you wear; diamonds offer clarity and purity, which can aid with your manifestations. Sapphires are linked to wisdom, royalty and protection, assisting you to connect to your inner wisdom. Amethysts, associated with spiritual power, can help to blast open your intuition.

The power of the Queen has been divinely given, yet with it comes a great responsibility to rule and safeguard the people of her kingdom. This archetype asks you to have sovereignty over your own life, encouraging you to take responsibility for your decisions and actions. Self-mastery involves understanding both your strengths and weaknesses and ruling your inner world with wisdom and grace.

*

Consider the power of a tiara, and let it perch upon your brow like a shimmering halo. One of Coco Chanel's style choices was her unconventional use of tiaras. Rather than confining these regal adornments to the head, Coco boldly wore them as necklaces, transforming symbols of aristocratic tradition into modern, wearable art.

> *Question: What is your relationship with power? Do you give it away? Do you wait for it to be given to you? Do you take it? Or is power something earned? Claim your personal power and authority. Declare your power, don't hide it – let your power be known.*

THE MINIMALIST

OPT FOR A NEUTRAL COLOUR PALETTE FOR AN INSTANT CLASSIC AND TIMELESS STYLE.

Regain mental clarity and focus by reducing external distractions. In order to detach from material and worldly attachments, strip everything back with a neutral colour palette. Honour the purity of form, shedding what does not serve your highest self. In the grace of minimalism, you will experience the freedom and lightness of being – alongside a neutral colour palette, strip away the excess and find beauty in the bare and unadorned. You will discover the profound peace that simplicity brings.

*

At Chanel they are renowned for their iconic neutral shades, which famously complement every skin colour – be it taupe, beige, blush or ivory hues. These colours will instantly give your outfit a sense of sophistication as they offer a polished and seamless look. Famous Chanel hues include "Ballerina", a delicate pink hue that offers a feminine and sophisticated look, and "Particulière", a soft taupe-grey known for its chic and understated energy.

Reflection: Embrace the art of less. Cultivate a space where only the essentials remain, creating a sanctuary of simplicity.

THE HIGH PRIESTESS

A DELIBERATE CHOICE OF HEAD AND FOOT ACCESSORIES BRIDGES A CONNECTION BETWEEN YOUR SPIRIT AND THE PHYSICAL WORLD.

Balance your connection to the celestial worlds above your head from dimensions unseen and land this connection with ease into the stability of the earth beneath your feet. Cultivate this connection by paying special attention to what you place atop your crown and what you place on the soles of your feet.

The High Priestess card in tarot is one of the most powerful in the deck, symbolizing intuition, mystery and inner wisdom. She wears a lunar headdress that holds a full moon, while a crescent moon rests at her feet, reflecting her mastery over the unconscious realms and her connections to the cycles of nature. Behind her, hidden beyond a veil not seen by all, lies a boundary between the seen and unseen worlds also representing the conscious and unconscious mind.

*

The House of Chanel's signature black and white palette echoes the duality of the High Priestess, who sits between a black and a white pillar, representing the perfect balance between light and dark, the conscious and unconscious, balancing opposites in perfect harmony.

Affirmation: "Every day, I am stepping into new opportunities that connect me to the joys of life."

Let the crescent moon inspire you to reflect on actionable steps that align with your deepest desires – reflect on small, manageable tasks that can help to build momentum and lead you forward. What is the single next step you can take towards your goal?

"TRUST THE PROCESS OF GETTING TO KNOW YOURSELF. LETTING GO LOOKS GOOD ON YOU."

THE SAGE

DRESS YOURSELF IN NAVY, A SHADE AS ANCIENT AS THE NIGHT – THE COLOUR OF WISDOM AND STRENGTH.

The Sage wears navy to represent the profound depths of their wisdom – a colour embodying sincerity and reliability, qualities only cultivated through time and experience. Navy mirrors the mystery and vastness of spaces that span great distances, like the depths of the oceans and the infinite night sky.

*

This timeless colour became a staple of the Chanel uniform for it holds a practical elegance. It is said that Coco Chanel's love for the French seaside, particularly the beaches of Deauville and Biarritz, heavily influenced her use of navy. Similar to black, navy is an adaptable choice that can effortlessly transition from day to night, supporting the lifestyle of the modern individual.

Guidance: In need of some advice? Instead of sending out a survey of your questions to others, turn your gaze inwards, for you hold all the answers you seek within.

To tap into your intuition, begin by repeating this affirmation: "I connect to the infinite wisdom I hold from this life and each of the past lives my soul has embodied." Follow this with your yes/ no question and notice if your body expands (this is your yes) or contracts (this is your no).

CONCLUSION

THE BLUEPRINT OF WHAT YOU WILL TAKE FORWARD

These archetypes exist in the collective unconscious of all people. They influence our perceptions and shape our relationships. Understanding and integrating these archetypes can provide insight into personal growth, relationship dynamics and the broader themes explored in each chapter.

Don't shy away from the archetype that has made itself known to you – its power, wisdom, and lessons are yours to claim. This archetype appears because there is a part of you that is found in this archetype ready to be seen and acknowledged – nudging you to align with your true self and how you wish to present yourself in the world.

My intention is to help you reimagine your relationship with the clothes that you wear by adding a ritualistic and intentional layer to the art of dressing. This book encourages you to make your wardrobe work harder for you. Instead of instinctively purchasing something new for every occasion, infuse an energetic shift into your wardrobe by transforming something you already own and resurrecting it with a new, powerful and concise energy.

My desire is to inspire you to weave in esoteric themes into your everyday via your clothes. By connecting your fashion choices to the mysticism of the "woo-woo" in a way that feels accessible, inspiring, empowering, and undeniably stylish, you can infuse your style with a deeper sense of meaning and reconnect to your magic.

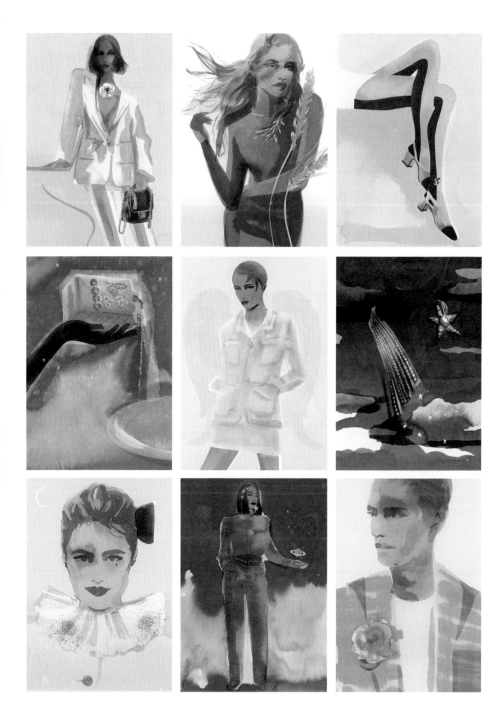

CHANEL'S LEGACY CONTINUED

Coco Chanel's legacy continues to have a profound impact on the fashion industry, reflecting her revolutionary approach to design, style and brand building. She founded her House in 1910, and continued working until she passed at the age of 88 years old in her room at the Ritz Hotel in 1971.

Twelve years after Coco's death, Chanel was revitalized by creative director Karl Lagerfeld, who took the helm in 1983. He added a younger edge to the collections while retaining and respecting the timeless legacy of the brand. Lagerfeld continued to innovate well beyond the typical retirement age until his passing at the age of 85 years old in 2019.

Following Lagerfeld's death, Virginie Viard, who had worked closely with Lagerfeld for over 30 years, was appointed Creative Director. Viard led the brand for five years, bringing her own interpretation of Chanel's iconic style while artfully preserving the House's core identity.

THANK YOUS

This *Fashion Oracle* book began with a deep dive into the archives of Chanel, guided by fashion stylist Zoë Sinclaire. Zoë's experience at Chanel runway shows, her visits to 31 rue Cambon, and her deep love for the brand were instrumental in shaping many of the details discussed in this book. My heartfelt thanks go to you, my dear friend, for your invaluable contribution during the image and research phase. Your keen eye and friendly ear were crucial in directing the stunning illustrations featured on these pages.

It's been an absolute joy to work with the incredibly talented fashion illustrator Joanna Layla. As with many aspects of my life, I wanted the process of creating this book to be filled with magic and ritual. Joanna graciously indulged me as I led us on a book-blessing ritual, opening all the chambers of our hearts, flooding them with cosmic light to ignite our creative fire and anchoring our intentions into the ether. Joanna has woven an extra touch of magic into the pages of this book with her incredible talent and enchanting illustrations.

Thank you to my brother Luke Tierney and his wife Lucrecia Tierney for being the cheerleaders I didn't know I needed, especially towards the end of the book writing process when I questioned every word I had put down on paper. You're both so special to me.

Thank you to my friend and fashion stylist Daisy Marlow for your editorial suggestions that helped shape this book, and to Alexandra Jones for your valuable support with additional image research. I've somehow attracted many earth angels throughout this book-writing process – I truly believe that the right people are placed on your path with the most perfect timing. This book has been an exercise in surrendering to this knowing and the magic of the universe. I'm more in love with my spiritual practice than ever.

My last thank you may surprise you. I am someone who often sees and connects with spirits, angels, ancestors and otherworldly beings. It is a part of my personal and professional life to be guided by these energies. I was, however, entirely startled when Karl Lagerfeld made his presence known to me as I began this book. Every project I do begins with a prayer and setting intentions, it was during this process that Lagerfeld shared his messages. He told me – with the authority of a parent explaining to a child – the importance of emphasizing the exquisite details of Coco Chanel's designs and the pioneering craftsmanship behind her collections. He stressed this book should celebrate Coco Chanel and highlight just how incredibly clever she was. Throughout this process, Lagerfeld has been a gentle and surprisingly nurturing guide, frequently reassuring me with his words: "C'est bien, Nieve" ("It's good, Nieve"). Phew!

When I asked Lagerfeld his thoughts at the end of this project, his final words to me were:

> "Ce livre offre une manière unique et ludique d'explorer la mode, comme un enfant curieux qui donne forme et couleur à son univers de jeu. C'est une méthode précise pour maîtriser l'énergie que l'on désire. J'aime cela." ("This book offers a unique and playful way to explore fashion, like a curious child given form and colour to play with. It's a precise method for mastering the energy one desires. I like that.")

Coco Chanel's energetic presence has been more elusive. She has never connected her energy directly with me, which feels entirely fitting given what I've come to understand about her personality through my research. I've felt her presence on a higher plane – her energy moves so quickly – at times she will pause and observe my ideas with a keen eye, but she never communicates her thoughts on my process.

ABOUT THE
AUTHOR

Nieve Tierney is a modern-day energy healer and Reiki Master. Before becoming a full-time healer, Nieve spent 15 years as a graphic designer and art director in the fashion industry, where her award-winning work involved collaborating with numerous high-profile luxury brands. Based in London, Nieve provides energy healing and coaching to a global roster of clients, notably Hollywood actors, high-profile executives, athletes and internationally renowned musicians.

Nieve believes: "Tending to your energetic body is one of the highest forms of self-care. When you consciously work with your energy you gain clarity about what energy belongs to you and what belongs to others. Choosing what to wear based on the energy you wish to embody shapes the energy you hold. Through conscious dressing, style becomes more than just fashion – it becomes an act of alchemy as you intentionally shift the vibration you hold through these choices."

@nievetierney
www.nievetierney.com

ABOUT THE ILLUSTRATOR

Joanna Layla is a London-based fashion illustrator and contemporary artist. Her unique style applies fluid brushstrokes and refined composition to fashion artwork. Communicating both beauty and concept, she has worked with numerous brands, including Miu Miu, adidas, the V&A and E.L.V. Denim.

   She shares: "When you take a sheet of watercolour paper, you can only see the light once you put the dark of the ink down on the page. It's the thing I love about ink. The light is revealed through the negative space of the ink. The negative space creates the light. It's magical."

@joannalayla
www.joannalayla.com

INDEX

SOURCES

27: *harpersbazaar.com/uk/fashion/fashion-news/news/a31524/the-world-according-to-coco-chanel/*
59: *harpersbazaar.com/fashion/designers/g32971271/best-coco-chanel-quotes/*
97: *harpersbazaar.com/fashion/designers/g32971271/best-coco-chanel-quotes/*
107: *wwd.com/fashion-news/shows-reviews/lagerfeld-talks-with-wwd-through-the-years-1203037647/*
127: *harpersbazaar.com/fashion/designers/g32971271/best-coco-chanel-quotes/*
163: *gq-magazine.co.uk/gallery/karl-lagerfeld-quotes*

Text © Nieve Tierney 2025
Design and layout © Headline Publishing Group Limited 2025

P200 PHOTO CREDIT: Photography: Philip Dunlop Studio, Styling: Daisy Marlow,
Photography Assistant: Luke Simmonds

Published in 2025 by Welbeck
An Imprint of HEADLINE PUBLISHING GROUP LIMITED

Cataloguing in Publication Data is available from the British Library

ISBN 9781035421930

Printed in China

Headline's policy is to use papers that are natural, renewable and recyclable
products and made from wood grown in well-managed forests and other
controlled sources. The logging and manufacturing processes are expected to
conform to the environmental regulations of the country of origin.

HEADLINE PUBLISHING GROUP LIMITED
An Hachette UK Company
Carmelite House
50 Victoria Embankment
London EC4Y 0DZ

The authorised representative in the EEA is Hachette Ireland,
8 Castlecourt Centre, Dublin 15, D15 XTP3, Ireland (email: info@hbgi.ie)

www.headline.co.uk
www.hachette.co.uk